499

THE
REBEL

PUBLISHING
HOUSE

Editors: Swami Yoga Pratap Bharati & Ma Yoga Sudha
Design and Typesetting: Ma Deva Harito
Production: Ma Deva Harito
Printing: Thomson Press (India) Limited
Published by The Rebel Publishing House Pvt. Ltd.,
50 Koregaon Park, Pune 411001 MS, India.
Copyright © 1997 Osho International Foundation
First edition: 1997
Reprinted: 1998
Reprinted: 1999
Osho® is a registered trademark of Osho International
Foundation, used under license.
ISBN 81-7261-019-X

THE
INNER
JOURNEY

OSHO

Spontaneous Talks Given by Osho
to Disciples And Friends at a
Meditation Camp in Ajol, Gujarat,
in India

IN LOVING GRATITUDE TO OSHO
SWAMI ANAND PRATIYAN

CONTENTS

INTRODUCTION

I remember an incident from my adolescence. Chandu-bhai, a friend of my father's, was visiting. He was a very quiet, contemplative type of seeker. We all used to respect him like a saint, though perhaps other people did not, because he was a householder and had not taken to the robe of a renunciate. But one day, while bringing tea for him, the cup fell out of my hand and broke in pieces. With a very natural and easy smile Chandubhai said, "Never mind, your attention must have been broken by a loss of equanimity." And I felt as if a *sutra*, one of life's precious clues, had fallen into my hands, although for me it was not a complete sutra because at that time my intellect was not mature enough to grasp its entire meaning. By the time I came to the age when I could have grasped something, Chandubhai was dead.

Then another incident happened. In Jodhpur, just near our house, lived an old widow, Jamnabai. She was declining in years, had dazzling white hair and her face was luminous with an amazing, peaceful radiance. She had only a buffalo, and her only source of income was from the sale of its milk and *ghee*. She was utterly un-educated. My father used to say, "If someone wants to learn *vedanta*, the true knowledge and how to live it, he should learn it from Jamnabai."

One day, after washing and bathing the buffalo,

Jamnabai was returning home holding the buffalo by a rope in one hand, supporting a pot full of water on her hip with the other hand, and balancing three pots full of water of successive sizes, one on top of the other, on her head. Meanwhile, Rambaba, who was always loudly chanting "Ram, Ram, Ram," could be seen coming from the opposite direction. Jamnabai greeted him with a nod of her head, and Rambaba began by saying, "Jamnabai, your whole life will be gone just in taking care of the buffalo. You should also pay some attention to the world of the beyond. Why don't you chant 'Ram, Ram,' like me?"

The answer that Jamnabai gave him left me astonished. She said, "Rambaba, do you see these three pots of water on my head? While greeting you, my awareness was still on them, so they don't get unbalanced and topple over. In the same way, I am busy all day long with my household chores, but my awareness remains constantly on the divine."

And I felt that some more of the sutra that had partially come into my hands at the time the teacup was broken was now being delivered to me.

Later, on Mahatma Gandhi's inspiration, I was translating the famous work *The Prophet* by Lebanon's great poet and philosopher Khalil Gibran into Hindi. While translating the chapters on love and on work, it felt as though the sutra had moved a little deeper.

It was then that a longing, a restlessness to complete the sutra sank deep into my heart, but no opportunity came to find the missing parts of it.

Thirty years passed by. One day I was sitting with my dear friend Mahipal when he mentioned Osho during our conversation and he handed me some of Osho's books. Reading them, it felt as if I had found a new ray of light. A new door was opened. It was as though here was the possible fulfillment of the incomplete sutra that I had been in search of for so many years.

And this is exactly what happened. In the very first chapter of this book, *The Inner Journey*, the whole sutra came into my hands:

"And the law which applies to the veena also applies to the veena of life. If the strings of life are too loose, then music does not arise; and if the strings of life are too tight, then too there is no music. One who wants to create the music of life has to see to it that the strings are not too tight or too loose."

Osho then puts forward the question, *"Where is that veena of life?"*

"Except for man's body, there is no other veena of life. And there are strings in the human body which should be neither too tight nor too loose. Only in balance does man enter into life's music. And to know that music is to know the soul. When a man comes to know his inner music, he comes to know his soul. And when he comes to know the music hidden within the whole, he comes to know God."

This sutra from Osho feels like a well-tested mathematical formula which, if applied correctly, will bring the correct answer to even the most complex of life's problems.

Each chapter of this book, *The Inner Journey*, goes on opening doors upon doors, and we go on diving deeper and deeper and deeper into our selves. The journey begins with the search for oneself, and ends with the attainment of love, of God.

In my opinion, Osho's revolutionary thinking is like that of the sages of the Upanishads trying to unveil the mysteries of existence, like a Socrates teaching the multitudes to use their wakeful intelligence, like a Lao Tzu suggesting to us to drop all artificiality and to return to our self-nature.

Kishori Raman Tandon
Mumbai, India
Poet, Author and Journalist

CHAPTER ONE

THE BODY: THE FIRST STEP

M Y   B E L O V E D   O N E S ,

In this first meeting of the meditation camp, I would like to talk about the first step for a meditator, a seeker. What is the first step? A thinker or a lover follow certain paths but a seeker has to travel on a totally different journey. For a seeker, what is the first step on the journey?

The body is the first step for a seeker – but no attention or thought has been given to it. Not only at certain times, but for thousands of years the body has been neglected. The neglect is of two kinds. Firstly, there are the indulgent people who have neglected the body. They have no experience of life other than eating, drinking and wearing clothes. They have neglected the body, misused it, foolishly wasted it – they have ruined their instrument, their *veena*.

If a musical instrument – for example a veena – is ruined, music cannot arise out of it. Music is an altogether different thing from the veena – music is one thing, the veena is another, but without the veena music cannot arise.

Those people who have misused the body through indulgence are one type, and the other type of people are those who have neglected the body through yoga and renunciation. They have tortured the body, they have suppressed it and they have been hostile towards it. And neither the people who have indulged the body nor the ascetics who have tortured the body have

3

understood its importance. So there have been two kinds of neglect and torture of the veena of the body: one by the indulgers and another by the ascetics. Both have done harm to the body.

In the West the body has been harmed in one way and in the East in another way, but we all are equal participants in harming it. People who go to brothels or to pubs harm the body in one way, and people standing naked in the sun or rushing into the forests harm the body in another way.

Only through the veena of the body can the music of life arise. The music of life is an altogether different thing from the body – it is totally different, something else – but only through the veena of the body is there a possibility of attaining to it. No proper attention has yet been given to this fact.

The first step is the body and the proper attention of the meditator towards the body. In this first meeting I want to talk to you about this point.

A few things need to be understood.

The first thing: the soul has a connection with the body at some centers – our life-energy comes from these connections. The soul is closely related to these centers; from them our life-energy flows into the body.

The seeker who is not aware of these centers will never be able to attain to the soul. If I ask you which is the most important center, which is the most important place in your body, you will probably point to your head.

Man's very wrong education has made the head the most important part of the human body. The head or brain is not the most important center of life-energy in man. It is like going to a plant and asking it what its most important and vital part is. Because the flowers can be seen at the top of the plant, the plant and everybody else will say that the flowers are the most important part. So although the flowers seem to be the most important, they are not; the most important part is the roots, which are not visible.

The mind is the flower on the plant of man, it is not the root. Roots come first, flowers come last. If the roots are ignored the flowers will wither away because they have no separate life of their own. If the roots are taken care of the flowers will be taken care of automatically; no special effort is needed to care for them. Looking at a plant it seems that the flowers are the most important part, and in the same way it seems that in man the mind is most important. But the mind is the final development in man's body, it is not the root.

Mao Zedong has written a memoir of his childhood. He wrote, "When I was small there was a very beautiful garden near my mother's hut. The garden was so beautiful, it had such beautiful flowers that people from distant places used to come to see them. Then my mother became old and fell sick. She was neither worried about her sickness nor about her old age. Her only worry was about what would happen to her garden."

Mao was young. He said to his mother, "Don't be worried, I will take care of your garden."

And Mao took care of the garden, working from the morning till the evening. After one month his mother got better, and as soon as she could walk a little she came into the garden. Seeing the condition of the garden she was shocked! The garden was ruined! All the plants had dried up. All the flowers had withered and fallen away. She became very much disturbed and said to Mao, "You idiot! You were in the garden the whole day. What did you do here? All these flowers are destroyed. The garden has withered away. All the plants are about to die. What were you doing?"

Mao started crying. He himself was troubled. Every day he had worked all day, but for some reason the garden went on drying out. He started crying and he said, "I took great care. I kissed each flower and loved it. I cleaned and wiped off the dust from each and every leaf, but I don't know what happened. I was worried also, but the flowers went on withering away, the leaves went on drying out and the garden went on dying!" His mother started laughing. She said, "You are an idiot! You don't know yet that the life of the flowers is not in the flowers and the life of the leaves is not in the leaves!"

The life of a plant is in a place that is not at all apparent to anyone: it is in the roots which are hidden beneath the ground. If one does not take care of those roots, the flowers and the leaves cannot be taken care of. Howsoever much they may be kissed, howsoever much they may be loved, howsoever much the dust on them may be cleaned, the plant will wither away. But if one does not bother about the flowers at all and takes care of the roots, the flowers will take care of themselves. The flowers come out of the roots, not the other way around.

If we ask somebody which is the most important part in a human body, then unknowingly his hand will point towards his head and he will say that his head is the most important. Or, if it is a woman, then maybe she will point towards her heart and say that the heart is the most important.

Neither the head nor the heart is the most important. Men have emphasized their heads and women have emphasized their hearts and the society based on this mixture has continuously been ruined every day, because neither of these parts are the most important part in a human body; both are very late developments. Man's roots are not in them.

What do I mean by the roots of man? Just as the plants have roots in the earth from which they draw their life-energy and life juices and live, similarly, in the human body there are roots at some point which draw life-energy from the soul. Because of this the body remains alive. The day those roots become feeble the body begins to die.

The roots of plants are in the earth, the roots of the human body are in the soul. But neither the head nor the heart is the place from where man is connected to his life-energy – and if we do not know anything about those roots then we can never enter the world of a meditator.

Then where are the roots of man? Perhaps you are not aware of the place. If even simple and common things are not given any attention for thousands of years they are forgotten. A child is born in the womb of a mother and grows there. Through which part is the child connected to its mother? Through the head or through the heart? No, it is connected through the navel. The life-energy is available to it through the navel – the heart and the mind develop later on. The life-energy of the mother becomes available to the child through the navel. The child is connected to his mother's body through his navel. From there the roots spread out into the mother's body and in the opposite direction, into his own body as well.

The most important point in the human body is the navel, after that the heart develops, and after that the mind. These are all branches which develop later. It is on them that the flowers blossom. Flowers of knowledge blossom in the mind, flowers of love blossom in the heart. It is these flowers which allure us, and then we think that they are everything. But the roots of man's body and his life-energy are in the navel. No flowers blossom there. The roots are absolutely invisible, they are not even seen. But the degeneration that has happened to human life in the past five thousand years is because we have placed all our emphasis either on the mind or on the heart. Even on the heart we have placed very little emphasis; most of the emphasis has gone to the mind.

From early childhood all education is an education of the mind, there is no education of the navel anywhere in the world. All education is of the mind, so the mind goes on growing larger and larger, and our roots go on becoming smaller and smaller. We take care of the mind because the flowers blossom there, so it becomes larger – and our roots go on disappearing. Then the life-energy flows more and more feebly, and our contact with the soul becomes weak.

Slowly, slowly we have even come to a point where man is saying, "Where is the soul? Who says there is a soul? Who says there is a God? We do not find anything." We will not find anything. One cannot find anything. If somebody searches all over the body of the tree and says, "Where are the roots? I cannot find anything" – then what he is saying is right. There are no roots anywhere on the tree. And we have no access to the place where the roots are; of that place we have no awareness. From early childhood all training, all education is of the mind, so our whole attention gets entangled and ends up focused on the mind. Then for our whole life we wander around the mind. Our awareness does not ever go below it.

The journey of a meditator is downwards, towards the roots. One has to descend from the head to the heart and from the heart to the navel. Only from the navel can anybody enter into the soul; before that one can never enter it.

Normally the movement of our life is from the navel towards the head. The movement of a seeker is exactly opposite: he has to descend from the head to the navel.

In these three days I will be talking to you and showing you, step by step, how to descend from the head to the heart and from the heart to the navel – and then how to enter the soul from the navel.

Today it is necessary to say a few things about the body.

The first thing to understand is that the center of man's life-energy is the navel. Only from there does the child acquire life; only from there do the branches and sub-branches of his life start spreading; only from there does he get energy; only from there does he get vitality. But our attention is never focused on that energy center – not even for a minute. Our focus is not on the system through which we get to know that energy center, that center of vitality. Instead our whole attention and our whole education is focused on the system that helps to forget it. That is why our whole education has gone wrong.

Our whole education is taking man slowly, slowly towards madness.

The mind alone will take man only towards madness.

Do you know that the more a country becomes educated, the more the number of mad people increases there? America has the largest number of mad people today. It is a matter of pride! It is proof that America is the most educated, the most civilized country. American psychologists say that if the same system continues for another hundred years, it will be difficult to find a sane man in America. Even today the minds of three out of four people are in a shaky condition.

In America alone, three million people are consulting psychoanalysts every day. Slowly, slowly in America the number of physicians is becoming less and psychoanalysts are increasing. The physicians also say that eighty percent of man's diseases are of the mind, not of the body. And as the understanding grows this percentage increases. First they used to say forty percent, then they started saying fifty percent, now they say that eighty percent of diseases are of the mind, not of the body. And I assure you that after twenty to twenty-five years they will say that ninety-nine percent of diseases are of the mind, not of the body. They will have to say so because our whole emphasis is on man's mind. The mind has become insane.

You have no idea how very delicate, very fragile and very subtle a thing the brain is. Man's brain is the most delicate machine in the world. So much stress is being imposed on this machine that it is a wonder that it does not break down completely and become mad! The whole burden of life is on the brain, and we have no idea how delicate a thing it is. We have hardly any idea of how fine and delicate the nerves in the head are which have to carry all the burden, all the anxiety, all the suffering, all the knowledge, all the education...the whole weight of life.

You may perhaps not know that in this small head

there are about seventy million nerves. Just by their number you can tell how tiny they are. There is no machine or plant more delicate than this. The fact that there are seventy million nerves in the small head of man shows how delicate it is. There are so many nerves in a single man's head that if they were spread out one after the other, they would encircle the whole earth.

In this small head there is such a subtle mechanism, such a delicate mechanism. In the past five thousand years all the stress of life has been placed on this delicate brain alone. The result was inevitable. The result is that the nerves have started breaking down, becoming insane, going mad.

The burden of thoughts cannot take man anywhere else other than into madness. Our whole life-energy has started moving around the brain.

A meditator has to bring this life-energy deeper, more downwards, more towards the center; he has to turn it back. How can it be turned back? To understand this we must understand something about the body – the first step.

The body is not seen as a vehicle for the spiritual journey or as a temple of the divine or as an instrument for discovering the center of life. The body is seen either from the point of view of indulgence or from the point of view of renunciation – but both of these approaches are wrong.

The path to whatsoever is great in life and whatsoever is worth attaining to is within the body and goes through the body.

The body should be accepted as a temple, as a spiritual path – and as long as this is not our attitude we are either indulgers or we are renouncers. In both cases our attitude towards the body is neither right nor balanced.

A young prince was initiated by Buddha. He had seen all kinds of pleasures in his life, he had lived only for pleasure. Then he became a *bhikshu*, a monk. All the other bhikshus were very much surprised. They said, "This person is becoming a bhikshu! He has never gone out of his palace, he has never walked without his chariot. The paths he used to walk on were covered with velvety carpets. Now he wants to become a beggar! What kind of madness is he thinking of doing?"

Buddha said that man's mind always moves between extremes – from one extreme to the other. Man's mind never stops in the middle. Just as a pendulum of a clock moves from one end to the other but never stays in the middle, in the same way the mind of man goes from one extreme to the other. Up to now this man had lived at one extreme – the indulgence of his body; now he wanted to live at the other extreme – the renunciation of his body.

And this happened. While all the bhikshus would walk on the highways, the prince, who had never walked anywhere except on the most valuable carpets, would walk on the pathways where there were thorns. When all the bhikshus would sit under the shadow of a tree, he would stand in the sun. When all the bhikshus

13

would eat once every day, he would fast one day and eat the next day. Within six months he became a skeleton, his beautiful body turned black and his feet became wounded.

After six months Buddha went to him and said, "Shrona!" – this was his name – "I want to ask you one thing. I have heard that when you were a prince, you were very good at playing the veena. Is it true?"

The bhikshu said, "Yes. People used to say that there was no one else who could play the veena like me."

Buddha said, "Then I have come to ask you one question – maybe you can answer it. My question is, 'If the strings of the veena are too loose, can music arise or not?'"

Shrona started laughing. He said, "What kind of question are you asking? Even children know that if the strings of a veena are too loose then music will not arise, because sound cannot be created on loose strings, one cannot pluck them. So music cannot arise out of loose strings."

Then Buddha said, "And if the strings are too tight?"

Shrona answered, "Music does not arise out of strings which are too tight either, because strings which are too tight break the moment they are touched."

So Buddha asked, "When does the music arise?"

Shrona said, "Music arises when the strings are in such a state that we can neither say that they are very tight nor can we say that they are very loose. There is a state when they are neither loose nor tight. There is a point in between, a midpoint: music arises only there.

And an expert musician checks the strings to see if they are too loose or too tight before he starts playing."

Buddha said, "Enough! I have received the answer. And I have come to tell you the same thing. Just as you were an expert at playing the veena, in the same way I have also become a master of playing the veena of life. And the law which applies to the veena also applies to the veena of life. If the strings of life are too loose then music does not arise, and if the strings of life are too tight then too there is no music. One who wants to create the music of life has first to see that the strings are not too tight or too loose."

Where is that veena of life?

Except for the body of man there is no other veena of life. And there are strings in the human body which should neither be too tight nor too loose. Only in that balance does man enter into music. To know that music is to know the soul. When a man comes to know his inner music within himself he comes to know the soul; and when he comes to know the music hidden within the whole he comes to know the divine.

Where are the strings of the veena of man's body? The first thing is: there are many strings in the mind which are very tight. They are so tight that music cannot arise from them. If somebody touches them, only madness arises and nothing else. And you are all living with the strings of your mind being very tight. For twenty-four hours a day you are keeping them tense, from morning till evening. And if somebody thinks that they may be relaxed at night, he is mistaken. Even during the night your mind is stressed and tense.

Previously we did not know what goes on in a man's mind during the night, but now machines have been invented. While you are sleeping the machine will go on reporting what your brain is doing inside.

At this time, in America and Russia, there are about a hundred laboratories testing what a man does in his sleep. About forty thousand people have been experimented upon while sleeping during the night. The results that have been found are very surprising. The results show that whatsoever a man does during the day, he does during the night. Whatsoever he does the whole day...if he runs a shop in the daytime, then even at night he is running the shop. If the mind worries the whole day, then it goes on worrying during the night. If it is angry during the day, then it remains angry during the night.

The night is the reflection of the whole day; it is its echo. Whatsoever happens in the mind during the day resounds as an echo during the night. Whatsoever has been left incomplete, the mind tries to complete it during the night. If you were angry and you did not express anger totally towards some person, if the anger was left incomplete or stuck, then the mind releases it at night. By completing the expression of anger the string of the veena tries to reach to the right state. If somebody has fasted during the day, then at night he eats in his dream. Whatsoever has been left incomplete during the day tries to be completed at night.

So whatsoever the mind does during the day, it does the same thing the whole night. For twenty-four hours the mind is tense; there is no rest. The strings of the mind are never relaxed. The strings of the mind are very tense – that is one thing.

And the second thing is: the strings of the heart are very loose. The strings of your hearts are not tight at all. Do you know something like love? You know anger, you know envy, you know jealousy, you know hatred. Do you know something like love? Perhaps you would say that you do – sometimes you love. Perhaps you would say that you hate and you also love. But do you know...? Can there be a heart which hates and also loves? It is the same as saying that a person is sometimes alive and sometimes dead! You cannot believe this because a man can either be alive or he can be dead; both these things cannot happen simultaneously. That a man is sometimes alive and sometimes dead is not possible; it is impossible. Either the heart knows only hate or the heart knows only love. There can be no compromise between the two. In a heart which has love, hatred becomes impossible.

There was a *fakir* woman named Rabiya. In the holy book which she used to read she had canceled one line, she had crossed out a line in it. Nobody crosses out lines in the holy books! – because what can one improve on in the holy books?

Another fakir came to stay with Rabiya. He read the book and he said, "Rabiya, somebody has destroyed your holy book! It has become unholy, one line has been crossed out in it. Who has crossed it out?"

Rabiya said, "I crossed it out."

The fakir was very shocked. He said, "Why did you cross out this line?" The line was: hate the Devil.

Rabiya said, "I am in a difficulty: from the day that love for God arose in me hate disappeared within me, so even if I want to I cannot hate. Even if the Devil comes in front of me, then too I will only be able to love him. I have no other choice – because before I can hate I need to have hate in me; before I can hate I must have hate in my heart. Otherwise, from where will I get it and how will I do it?"

Love and hate cannot coexist in the same heart. These two things are as contrary as life and death: they cannot exist together in the same heart.

Then what is that which you call love? When there is less hate you call it love, when there is more hate you call it hate. They are lesser and greater proportions of hate itself. There is no love there at all. The mistake happens because of the degrees. Because of the degrees you may mistakenly think that cold and heat are two different things. They are not two different things: heat and cold are gradations of the same thing. If the ratio of heat becomes less, then something starts feeling cold; if the ratio of heat becomes more, then the same thing starts feeling hot. Cold is another form of heat. They seem to be opposite, different, opposed to each other, but they are not. They are condensed and non-condensed forms of the same thing.

You know hate in the same way: the less condensed form of hate you understand as love, and the very condensed form of hate you understand as hate – but love is in no way a form of hate. Love is a totally different thing from hate – love has no relation to hate.

The strings of your heart are totally loose. The music of love does not arise from those loose strings – neither does the music of bliss. Have you ever known bliss in your life? Can you say about some moment that it was a moment of bliss and that you recognized and experienced bliss? It is difficult to say with authenticity that you have ever known bliss.

Have you ever known love? Have you ever known peace? It is also difficult to say anything about them.

What do you know? You know restlessness. Yes, sometimes the restlessness is of a lesser degree – which you take to be peace. Actually, you are so restless that if the restlessness becomes a little less it gives an illusion of peace. A man is sick: when the sickness becomes a little less, he says that he has become healthy. If the sickness that is surrounding him becomes a little less, he thinks that he has become healthy. But what is the relation of health to sickness? Health is a totally different thing.

Health is a completely different thing. Very few of us are able to know health. We know more sickness, we know less sickness, but we do not know health. We know more restlessness, we know less restlessness, but we do not know peace. We know more hate, we know less hate. We know more anger, we know less anger....

You may think that anger only happens sometimes. This idea is false – you are angry twenty-four hours of the day! Sometimes it is more, sometimes it is less, but you are angry for twenty-four hours of the day. With just a little opportunity the anger will start surfacing. It is in search of an opportunity. The anger is ready inside; it is only in search of an opportunity on the outside to give you an excuse to be angry. If you become angry without an excuse, then people will think you are mad. But if opportunities are not given to you, you will start becoming angry even without any reason. Perhaps you do not know this.

For example, a person can be locked in a room, provided with every facility and asked to note down any changes which happen to his mind. When he notes them down he will find that without any reason sometimes he feels good in that closed room, sometimes he feels bad; sometimes he becomes sad, sometimes he becomes happy; sometimes he feels angry, sometimes he does not feel angry. There are no excuses there, the situation in the room is constantly the same – but what is happening to him? That is why man is so afraid of aloneness – because in aloneness there are no excuses from the outside; he will have to assume all the things are within himself. Any person kept in isolation cannot remain healthy for more than six months, he will become mad.

A fakir told an Egyptian emperor about this but the

emperor did not believe him. So the fakir asked him to find the healthiest person in his city and to put him in isolation for six months. The city was searched. A healthy young man, who was happy in every way – was just married, had a child, was earning well, was very happy – was brought to the emperor. The emperor told him, "We will not give you any trouble. We are just doing an experiment. Your family will be taken care of – food, clothing, and every arrangement will be made for them. It will be a better situation for them than it will be for you. You will have all comforts but for six months you will have to live alone."

He was locked up in a big house. He was given every facility – but it was so lonely! Even the man who was guarding did not know his language, so they could not speak to each other. Within only two or three days the man started becoming nervous. He had every comfort, there were no hardships whatsoever: food was available at the right time, he could go to sleep at the right time. Because it was a royal palace, every facility was available and there were no difficulties whatsoever. Sitting there he could do whatsoever he wanted to do. The only thing was that he could not talk to anybody, he could not meet anybody. Within just two or three days he began to feel uneasy and after eight days he started shouting, "Take me out of here! I don't want to stay here!"

What was the problem? – the problems had started coming from within. The problems that until the day before he had thought were coming from the outside, he now found, in his aloneness, were coming from the inside.

Within six months the man became mad. After six months, when he was taken out, he had gone completely mad. He had started talking to himself, he had started cursing himself, he had started getting angry with himself, he had started loving himself. Now the other was not present. After six months he was taken out as a madman. It took six years for him to be cured.

Any one of you would become mad. Other people give you opportunities, hence you do not become mad. You find an excuse: "This man has abused me, therefore I am filled with anger." Nobody gets filled with anger by someone abusing him. The anger is present within; the abuse is only an opportunity for it to come out.

A well is full of water: if you drop a bucket in the well and pull it out, water comes out of the well. If there is no water in the well, then howsoever many times you drop the bucket in nothing can come out. The bucket by itself has no power to get water out – first, there should be water in the well. If there is water in the well then a bucket can draw water; if there is no water in the well then the bucket cannot draw water.

If there is no anger within you, if there is no hate within you, then no power in the world can bring anger or hate out of you. During these moments in between, when no one drops a bucket in the well, one can maintain an illusion that there is no water in the well. When someone does drop a bucket into it, water can be drawn; but when the well is not being used we would be mistaken to think that now there is no water in it. In the same way, if nobody gives us the opportunity, then no anger or hate or envy comes out of us. But do not think that there is no water in your well! The water is there in the well, and it is waiting for someone to come with a bucket and take it out. But we think these empty, in-between moments are moments of love, of peace. This is a mistake.

Always, after any war in the world, people say that now there is peace. But Gandhi said, "In my understanding it is not like that. Either there is war or there is preparation for war; peace never comes. Peace is a deception."

Just now there is no war happening in the world; the second world war has ended and we are waiting for the third world war. If we say that these are days of peace, we are wrong. These are not days of peace – these are days of preparation for the third world war. All over the world the preparations for a third world war are going on. Either there is war or there is preparation for war. The world has never seen a peaceful day for as long as it has existed.

Within man also there is either anger or there is preparation for anger – man does not know a state of non-anger. There is restlessness – either it surfaces or it is preparing to surface. If you think that the moments of preparation within are moments of peace, you are mistaken.

The strings of your heart are very loose: only anger comes out of them, only distortion and disharmony come out of them. No music can arise. If the strings of your mind are too tight then madness arises out of them, and if the strings of your heart are too loose then only anger, enmity, envy and hate arise out of them. The strings of your heart should be a little tighter so that love can arise out of it, and the strings of your mind should be a little looser so that a wakeful intelligence can arise out of it, not insanity. If both these strings become balanced there is a possibility for the music of life to arise.

So we will discuss two things: one is how to relax the strings of the mind and the other is how to tighten, to create a tension in the strings of the heart. The method to do this is what I call meditation.

If these two things happen, then the third thing can happen: then it is possible to descend to the real center of your life – the navel. If music arises in both these centers it becomes possible to move within. That music itself becomes a boat to take you deeper. The more harmonious the personality, the more music is arising within, the deeper you can descend. The more disharmony there is within the more you will remain shallow, the more you will remain on the surface.

In the coming two days we will discuss these two points – not only discuss them but also experiment with how we can bring these strings of the veena of life into balance.

The three points that I have just told you about have

to be kept in mind, so that you can connect them with the things I will now say to you.

The first thing: man's soul is connected neither to the mind nor to the heart – man's soul is connected to his navel. The most important point in a man's body is the navel; it is the center. The navel is not only in the center of man's body but also in the center of life. A child is born through it and his life ends through it. And for the people who discover truth, it is the navel which becomes the door.

You may not be aware that you breathe all day with your chest but at night your breathing starts coming from the navel. The whole day your chest goes up and down, but at night when you are asleep your belly starts moving up and down. You must have seen a small child breathing: the chest of a small child is not moving, it is his belly that is moving up and down. Small children are still very close to the navel. As a child starts growing he starts breathing only from the chest and the reverberations of the breath no longer reach the navel.

If you are going along a road, riding a bicycle or driving a car and suddenly an accident happens, you will be surprised to notice that the first impact will be on the navel, not on the mind or the heart. If a man suddenly attacks you with a knife the first tremor will be felt at the navel, not anywhere else. Even right now if you suddenly become afraid, the first tremor will be felt at the navel. Whenever there is a danger to life, the first tremors are felt at the navel because the navel is the center of life. The tremors will not happen anywhere else. The sources of life are connected from there, and because our attention is not at all on the navel man is left hanging in limbo. The navel center is totally sick, there is no attention paid to it – and there are no arrangements for its development.

Some kind of arrangements should be made to help develop the navel center. Just as we have created schools and colleges to develop the mind, in the same way some arrangement is absolutely necessary to develop the navel center – because there are certain things which develop the navel center and there are certain things which do not develop it.

As I said, if a situation of fear arises then it is felt first of all at the navel center. So the more one practices fearlessness, the more healthy one's navel will become; and the more one practices courage, the more one's navel center will develop. The more fearlessness grows, the stronger and healthier the navel will be – and the deeper ones contact with life. That is why all the great meditators of the world have considered fearlessness to be an essential quality in a seeker; fearlessness has no other significance. The significance of fearlessness is that it makes the navel center totally alive; it is absolutely instrumental in the total development of the navel.

We will talk about it step by step.

It is essential to give maximum attention to the navel center, so it is necessary to shift the attention slowly, slowly from the mind center and from the heart center so that it can go downwards and enter deeper and deeper. For this we will do two meditation experiments, one in the morning and one at night. I will explain the morning experiment to you, and then for fifteen minutes we will sit and do that meditation.

If consciousness is to be brought downwards from the mind, it is necessary to keep the mind completely relaxed. But we keep the mind tense all the time. We have forgotten that we go on keeping it tense: it is totally tense and we are not aware of it. So first it is necessary to allow it to relax.

Now when we sit for the meditation, there are three things....

The first thing: the whole mind has to be relaxed, so calm and relaxed that it is not doing anything. But how will you know that it is relaxed? If we close the fist very tightly we become aware that all the muscles are very tense. Then when we open the fist we become aware that all the muscles have become loose and relaxed. Because our minds are tense all the time, we do not even know what it is to be tense and what it is to be relaxed. So we will do one thing: first we will make the mind as tense as we can, then we will suddenly relax it – and you will realize what the difference between the mind being tense and being relaxed is.

Now, when we sit for meditation, for one minute make the mind as tense as you can, give it as much stress as you can. And then I will say, "Now let it relax" – then let it totally relax. Gradually you will come to know what it is to be tense and what it is to be relaxed.

You should be able to feel it, it should become your experience. And then you will be able to relax it more and more. So the first thing is to relax the mind totally.

Along with the mind the whole body has to be relaxed. One has to sit so comfortably that there is no tension or stress anywhere in the body. There should be no weight anywhere on the body. Then what will you do? The moment you allow everything to be relaxed the birds start singing, there is the sound of the watermill, somewhere a crow may cry, somewhere there will be some other sound.... You will start hearing all these sounds because the more relaxed the mind is, the more sensitive it will become. You will start hearing and feeling every little thing. You will also start hearing your own heartbeat and hearing and feeling the coming and going of your breath.

Then, sitting silently, one should experience quietly all that is happening around and do nothing else. You are hearing sounds? – listen to them silently. A bird is singing – listen to it silently; the breath is moving in and out – go on watching it silently: nothing else has to be done. You do not have to do anything from your side because as soon as you do, the mind will start becoming tense.

You have just to go on sitting in a state of relaxed awareness. Everything is happening on its own, you are simply listening to it quietly. And you will be amazed that as you listen silently, a deeper silence will start arising within you. The more deeply you listen, the more the silence will go on growing. Within ten minutes you will find that you have become an extraordinary center of silence, everything has become peaceful.

So we will do this technique as the first experiment of the morning. The first thing: you will make your mind totally tense. When I tell you to make the mind completely tense, then close your eyes and make your mind as tense as you can. Then I will tell you to let it relax: then let it relax, go on letting it relax.... In the same way also let the body relax. The eyes will be closed, and sitting silently, listen quietly to whatever sounds you hear. For ten minutes you have to simply listen silently – nothing else has to be done. In these ten minutes, for the first time you will start feeling that a stream of silence has started flowing and your life-energy has started descending within. It will start sinking downwards from the head.

You will have to sit a little farther apart from each other. Nobody should touch anybody else. Some people can come to the back on the lawn. The people who are familiar with this morning meditation, those who have attended previous meditation camps can sit at the back on the lawn, so that those who are new can listen. That way if I want to say something to them, if I want to give any instruction to them, they can hear. Those who are acquainted should go to the back so that the new people can sit in the front. Yes, old friends can go to the back and new friends can come forward. Some friends can come up here, some friends can come behind so that you can hear. Nobody should sit touching anybody else. Nobody should touch the other. You are still touching each other! Move a little apart! Move a little further! Sit on the sand!

First of all close your eyes softly. Very softly, close your eyes. There should be no strain on the eyes. It is not that you close them forcibly: drop the eyelids slowly, there should be no weight on the eyes. Close your eyes. Yes, close your eyes, close them softly.

Now allow the whole body to be relaxed and make only the mind tense. Put as much tension as you can on the mind, give it as much stress as you can, stress the whole mind. Force yourself to make the whole mind tense. Make it tense with all the strength you have. Make it tense with all your strength but let the whole body relax. Give all the energy to the mind so that the mind is totally tense – just like a closed fist with all the muscles tense. For one minute keep it tense in every way. Don't allow it to be loose, make it totally tense. Make it as tense as possible. Make the mind within tense in every way. Keep it tense. Make it tense with your full strength, to a climax. With whatever strength you have make it so totally tense that when you let it relax, it can be totally relaxed. Make it tense! Tense it!

Now let it completely relax. Allow it to relax totally. Let the mind be relaxed totally. Release all the tension. A relaxation will start happening inside. You will feel inside that something has dropped, some tension has disappeared, something has become peaceful. Let it relax totally, just relax....

And the sounds which are all around – the wind passing through the leaves, some birds singing – sitting silently, quietly listen to all these sounds. Just listen.

Keep listening to the sounds all around. As you listen the mind will become even more silent, even more silent...listen! Listen silently, totally relaxed. Keep listening. For ten minutes just become a listening.... Go on listening and the mind will start becoming silent.... Go on listening silently, just listening; the mind will become silent. A silence will start arising within you on its own. You just listen...go on listening – the mind is becoming silent, the mind is becoming totally silent. The mind is becoming silent. Go on listening in silence, the mind is becoming silent....

THE HEAD, THE HEART, THE NAVEL

CHAPTER TWO

THE HEAD, THE HEART, THE NAVEL

M Y   B E L O V E D   O N E S ,

This afternoon I would like to discuss a few more points relating to the real center of the body. A few questions have also been asked about this.

Neither the head nor the heart – the navel is the most important and basic center of man's life.

Man has developed according to his mind, so the direction, the flow of his life has gone wrong. In the past five thousand years we have educated and developed only the mind, only the intellect. The results have been very harmful. The results are that almost every human being is on the verge of madness – a little push and anyone can become mad. The mind is almost on the verge of a breakdown: a little push and the mind can collapse.

It is also a surprising thing that in the last half century, within the last fifty years, almost all the greatest thinkers of the world have gone mad.

In the West in the last half century there has hardly been a single thinker who did not experience some kind of madness. Great poets, great thinkers, great philosophers, great scientists have all been found to be suffering from some kind of madness. And slowly, slowly, as more and more of humanity is becoming educated, the symptoms of madness are also reaching the common people.

If a new man is to be created, it is absolutely essential to change the center of man's life. If that center is closer to the navel instead of to the head, it will be closer to the life-energy.

Why do I say this? In this context, it is necessary to understand a few more things. The child which develops in the mother's womb, the foetus which develops, is connected to the mother through the navel. The life-energy of the mother flows into the child through the navel itself. The life-energy of the mother is a very unknown, a very mysterious flow of electricity which nourishes the whole being of the child through his navel. Then the child separates from the mother, he is born. Immediately after his birth his navel cord has to be cut and the separation from his mother begins.

It is absolutely necessary for the child to separate from the mother, otherwise he cannot have any life of his own. The child that has grown in the mother and has been one with her body has to separate from her at a certain point. This separation happens by cutting the connection which he had with her at the navel. When this connection is cut, the life-energy that he was getting through the navel stops totally. His whole being starts trembling. His whole being starts asking for that flow of life-energy that he was getting until yesterday but which today has suddenly stopped.

The pain that the child feels, his crying after his birth, is not because of hunger: it is because of the pain of being separated and disconnected from the life-energy. His connection with the whole life-energy has been broken; the source from which he obtained life until yesterday has now gone. The child struggles for life –

and if the child does not cry the doctors or the people who know will say that something has gone wrong. If the child does not cry it means that he will not be able to survive. That he has not felt that he has been separated from the life-energy can mean only one thing: that he is close to his death and will not survive. That is why every effort is made to make the child cry. His crying is absolutely necessary because if he is to live, he should know that he has been separated from the life-energy. If he does not know, he is in great danger.

And that is when the child tries to reconnect his life-energy in a new way. And it is through the mother's milk that his life-energy reconnects. So a child's second connection is with the heart. Together with his mother's heart, his own heart center also slowly starts developing and the navel center is forgotten. The navel center has to be forgotten because it has been disconnected, it is no longer related to him. And the energy which he was receiving through the navel he now starts receiving through his mouth. He is again united with the mother. Another circuit is created and through it he becomes connected.

You will be surprised to know that if a child does not get his nourishment through his mother's milk, if he is not fed with his mother's milk, then his life-energy remains weak forever. He can be fed milk in other ways also, but if he does not regularly receive the warm touch of his mother's heart, then his life becomes frustrated forever and the possibility of his living a long life is reduced forever. Those children who are not fed on mother's milk can never attain to much bliss and silence in their lives.

The whole younger generation in the West, and gradually in India also, is becoming filled with great rebellion. The deepest reason for this, the root cause, is that Western children are not being fed on mother's milk. Their respect for life and their relation to life is not full of love. From their very childhood their life-energy has received many shocks and they have become unloving. In those shocks, in the separation from their mother, they have become separated from life itself – because for a child there is primarily no other life than his mother.

All over the world, wherever women are becoming educated, they do not like to raise children close to them – and the effect has been extremely harmful. In tribal societies children are fed on mother's milk for a long time. The more a society becomes educated, the earlier the children are weaned from their mother's milk. The sooner the children are separated from their mother's milk, the more difficulty they will have in experiencing peace in their own lives. A deep restlessness will prevail in their lives from the very beginning. On whom will they take revenge for this restlessness? The revenge will be taken on the parents themselves.

All over the world children are taking revenge on their parents. On who else will they take revenge? They themselves do not know what kind of reaction is happening within them, what kind of rebellion is arising within them, what kind of fire is arising within them. But unconsciously, deep within, they know that this rebellion is the result of being separated from their mother too soon. Their hearts know this but their intellects do not. The result is that they will take revenge on their mothers and fathers – they will take revenge on everyone.

The child who is against his mother and father can never be in favor of God. There is no possibility that he can be in favor of God because the first feelings which arise in him towards God are those which arise towards his mother and father.

It is not without reason that all over the world God is called 'the father'. It is not without reason that God is seen as an image of one's father. If the first experiences in a child's life are of trust, gratitude and reverence towards his mother and father, only then will the same experiences develop towards God, otherwise not.

As soon as he is born a child is immediately separated from his mother. His second source of life-energy is related to the heart of his mother. But at a certain point a child will have to separate from his mother's milk too.

When does the right time come? It does not come as early as we think. Children should remain close to their mother's heart a little longer if their love and heart are to develop rightly throughout their lives. They are forced to separate very early. A mother should not separate the child from her milk, she should allow the child to separate on his own. At a certain point the child will separate on his own. For the mother to force the separation is just like taking the baby out of the womb after four or five months, instead of allowing him to come out after nine months. It is just as harmful when the mother separates her child from her milk before he himself decides to give it up because then the second center, the heart center of the child, also does not develop rightly.

While we are talking about this I would like to tell you something more. You will be surprised to hear it. Why is it that all over the world, the part of the woman's body to which men are attracted the most is her breasts? These are all children who were separated very early from their mother's milk! In their consciousness, somewhere deep inside, a desire has remained to be close to a woman's breasts. It has not been fulfilled – there is no other reason, there is no other cause. In tribal societies, in primitive societies where the children remain close to the mother's breasts long enough, men have no such attraction towards the breasts.

But why are your poems, your novels, your movies, your dramas, your pictures all centered around the breasts of women? They have all been created by men who, in their childhood, could not remain close to their mother's breast long enough. That desire is left unfulfilled and now it starts arising in new forms. Now pornographic pictures are being created, pornographic books and pornographic songs are being written. Now men harass women on the streets and throw stones at them. You create all these stupidities and then later on complain about them and try to get rid of them.

It is very necessary for the child to remain close to his mother's breasts long enough for his mental, his physical and his psychological growth to take place rightly. Otherwise his heart center will not develop properly: it remains immature, undeveloped, stuck. And when the heart center remains undeveloped then an impossible thing starts happening: the work which the heart could not complete, which the navel could not complete, the person tries to complete with his mind. This effort brings even more trouble, because each center has its own function and each center can only do its own work; it cannot do the work of other centers.

Neither the navel nor the mind can do the work of the heart. But as soon as the child is separated from the mother he has only one center left on which the whole burden falls – this is the mind center. Education, teaching, schools and colleges are all arranged for the mind center. Then only those people whose minds are more developed and capable make progress in life. A race begins, and they attempt to do all the work of their lives with the mind.

The love of a person who loves through his mind will be false – because the mind has nothing to do with love. Love can only happen through the heart, not through the mind. But the heart center is not properly developed so you start using the mind. You even think about love! Love has nothing to do with thinking, but in you even love is expressed as thinking. That is why there is so much sexuality all over the world.

Sexuality has only one meaning: it means that the

mind is being used to do the work of the sex center. When sex enters the mind the whole of life is destroyed – and now all over the world sex has entered the mind.

The sex center is the navel, because the greatest energy of life is sex: birth comes through it, life comes through it, the growth of life comes through it. But your navel centers are undeveloped so you are using other centers for its functions.

There is sex in animals but not sexuality, so even the sex of animals has a beauty, a joy.

The sexuality of man is ugly because sex has become a thought process in his mind – he even thinks about sex.

A person can eat a meal, eating is very good, but if someone thinks about food for twenty-four hours a day then he is mad. Eating is absolutely right, it is very necessary, one has to eat, but if somebody thinks about food for twenty-four hours a day then this person's centers have become disturbed – he is using his mind to do the work of his stomach. But food can neither reach the mind nor can the mind digest it. The mind can only think, can only contemplate. The more the mind thinks about food the more the work of the stomach will be wasted; it will become disturbed. Try sometime to digest your food by thinking!

Usually you eat your food and then you don't think about it. The food enters the stomach by itself and the stomach does the work of digesting it. It is an unconscious center. It does its job, you don't have to think about it. But some day be alert and think about it: now the food has reached the stomach, now it is getting digested, now this is happening, now that is happening.... You will find that on that day digesting your food has become impossible. The more thinking enters, the more there will be a disturbance in the unconscious process of the stomach. Such incidents rarely happen with food – except with those people who are obsessed with fasting.

If a person fasts for no reason, then gradually food will enter his thoughts. He will not eat, he will fast – but he will be thinking about food. This thinking is even more dangerous than eating. Eating is certainly not dangerous. Food is very essential for life, but to think about food is a sickness. When a person starts thinking about food all growth in his life will stop. He will be obsessed with these futile thoughts.

This is what has happened with sex: we have forcibly shifted it from its proper center and now we are thinking about it.

In this way you have gradually handed over the functions of the three important centers of your life to the mind. It is just as if a man were to try to listen with his eyes or see with his mouth. It is as if a man were to try to see or taste with his ears. You would say that this man is mad because the eye is the mechanism for seeing and the ear is the mechanism for hearing. The ear cannot see, the eye cannot hear. If you try to do things in this way, the final result will be chaos.

In the same way man has three centers. The center

of life is the navel, the center of feeling is the heart and the center of thinking is the mind. Thinking is the outermost of these three centers. The next center, deeper, is of feeling, and even deeper than that is the center of being.

You may think that if the heart stops then the life-energy will also stop. But now scientists have come to the conclusion that although the heart may have stopped beating, the person can continue to live as long as it can be restarted within six minutes. After the connection with the heart has ended, the life center at the navel remains active for six more minutes. If within those six minutes the heart can be restarted or a new heart be transplanted, the person can continue to live and there will be no need for him to die. But if life has gone from the navel center, then nothing will be achieved by putting in a new heart. The deepest and most basic center within us is the navel. So this morning I have talked a little about this navel center.

The humanity we have created so far is upside-down. It is as if man is standing on his head, doing *shirshasana*. A person doing shirshasana is standing on his head with his feet in the air. If a man were to do shirshasana for twenty-four hours, what condition would he be in? You can understand! He would certainly go mad. He is already mad, otherwise he would not stand on his head for twenty-four hours; he has no reason to. But in your lives you have reversed things – you are all standing on your heads! You have made the head the basis of your lives. Thinking and contemplating have become the basis of life.

Authentic religion says that thinking and contemplating are not the basis of life – to become free from thinking and contemplating, to become thoughtless should be the basis. But you live by thinking and contemplating and you try to decide how to live your life by thinking and contemplating. Because of this, all your ways have gone astray. By thinking and contemplating nothing can be decided – food is not digested by your thinking, blood does not flow in your veins by your thinking, your breath does not move by your thinking.

Have you ever considered that no significant process of life is related to your thinking? In fact, all the processes of life slow down and become disturbed by too much thinking. That is why every night you need to get lost into a deep sleep, so that all your processes can function properly without your hindering them, and then in the morning you can feel fresh again. The very survival of a person who cannot lose himself in deep sleep is at stake, because thinking continuously disturbs the basic processes of your life. So for a little while nature drowns you in deep sleep, it takes you into a state of unconsciousness to where all thinking stops and your real centers become active.

There is also a relationship between your real centers. For example, I can be related to you through your intellect. My thoughts may seem right to you, my thoughts may seem impressive to you – then there will be an intellectual relationship between you and me.

This is the most shallow kind of relationship, but the intellect does not form any deeper relationship.

Deeper kinds of relationships are those of the heart, of love – but the relationships of love do not happen through thinking. The relationships of love happen totally unknowingly, without your thinking. And even deeper are the relationships of life which operate through the navel, not through the heart. They are even more indescribable. It is difficult to even define what kind of relationships they are because you do not know this dimension at all.

I told you earlier that the life-force of the mother activates the navel of the child. A kind of electricity continuously moves between the mother's navel and the child's navel. Then throughout his life, whenever that child goes near a woman from whom the same kind of electricity as his mother's is flowing, he will unconsciously feel a certain relationship. And he will not understand at all what kind of relationship he has started to feel or why. We have been calling this unknown relationship love. We are not able to recognize it, hence we call it 'blind' – love *is* blind. Just as the ears cannot see, the tongue cannot smell, and the eye cannot taste, in this way love is blind because it is arising from levels which are so deep that it becomes difficult for us to understand the reasons for it.

With some people you suddenly feel a strong repulsion, you feel you want to get away from them. And you do not understand the reason for wanting to get away from them. Why do you want to get away from them? If your electricity and their electricity – which is affected by the navel – is opposite, then without understanding it you will have to get away. It will seem to you as if something is forcing you to leave them.

But sometimes you suddenly feel pulled towards a person and you don't understand why; there seems to be no reason for it. Your electricity and his electricity are perceived to be closer, similar, of the same type, connected with each other – that is why you are having such an experience.

There are three types of relationships in a man's life. There are relationships of the intellect, which cannot be very deep. The relationship between a teacher and a student is this type of relationship. There are relationships of love, which are deeper than the intellect. The relationships between a mother and child, between brothers, between husband and wife are these types of relationships: they arise from the heart. Then there are even deeper relationships that arise from the navel. I call the relationships that arise from the navel 'friendships'. They go deeper than love. Love can end: friendship never ends. Tomorrow we may hate the people we love today – but someone who is a friend can never become an enemy. If he becomes an enemy, then know that there was no friendship in the first place. The relationships of friendship are of the navel – they are relationships of deeper and unknown realms.

This is why Buddha did not tell people to love each other. He talked about friendship. He had a reason for doing this – he said that there should be friends in your life. Somebody even asked Buddha, "Why do you not call it love?"

And Buddha replied, "Friendship is a much deeper thing than love. Love can end, friendship never ends."

Love binds, friendship gives freedom. Love can enslave somebody. It can possess, it can become a master. Friendship does not become someone's master, it does not hold anyone back. It does not imprison, it frees. Love becomes a bondage because the lovers insist that the other should not love anyone else but them.

Friendship has no such insistence. One man can have thousands of friends, millions of friends, because friendship is a very vast, very deep experience. It arises from the deepest center of life. That is why friendship ultimately becomes the greatest way to take you towards the divine. Someone who is a friend to all will sooner or later reach to the divine because his relationships are happening with everyone's navel center. And some day or other, he is bound to become related to the navel center of the universe.

One's relationships in life should not be merely intellectual, they should not be only heartful – they should be deeper, they should be of the navel.

For example, nowhere in the world is it clear – sooner or later it will become clear, sooner or later we will come to know – that we are connected with very far-away sources of life-energy which we cannot see. We know that the moon is very far away, yet it has some unknown influence on the ocean: the ocean rises and falls with the moon. We know that the sun is very far away, but it is connected to life through some invisible threads: the sun rises in the morning and a revolution happens in life! All that was sleeping, all that was lying as if dead, all that was unconscious starts becoming conscious. Something sleeping starts awakening, flowers start blossoming, birds start singing. An invisible flow from the sun leaves its influence on us.

There are other more invisible sources of life-energy which reach to us in this way: they manage our lives continuously. Not only the sun, not only the moon, not only the stars in the sky, but life itself has a flow of energy which is not seen by us anywhere and which continuously influences and manages our centers. The more receptive our center is, the more this energy can influence our lives. The less receptive our center is, the less this energy will be able to influence it.

The sun rises, the flower blossoms – but if we raise a wall around the flower and the sunlight does not reach the flower then the flower will not blossom, it will wither away. Behind closed walls the flower will wither away. The sun cannot forcibly enter and open the flower. The flower has to be willing, it has to be ready. The flower must give the sun the opportunity to come and open it.

The sun cannot go in search of a single flower, looking to see which flower is hiding behind a wall so that it can reach it. The sun does not even know about the flowers. It is all an absolutely unconscious life process: the sun rises, the flowers blossom. If a flower is enclosed within a wall it will not blossom, it will wither away and die.

Life-energy is flowing from all directions but those whose navel centers are not open will be deprived of that flow. They will not even know about it. They will not even realize that this energy was there and could have affected them, that there was something hidden within them which could have been opened. They will not even know this. This flowering of the navel which since ancient days has been called a lotus, is called a lotus because it has the possibility of opening – some life-energy may open it. One needs some preparation for this. For this, our center should be available to the open sky and we should give our attention to it. Then the life-energy which is available to us can reach the navel center and give it life. I have told you a few things about it this morning.

How will it be possible, how can it become possible for the center of your life to become a blossoming flower so that the invisible energy streams coming from all around can make connections with it? In what way will it happen? There are a few things I have remembered which I will talk to you about now, tonight, so that tomorrow we can talk about the second point.

The first point: your breathing.... The deeper it is, the more you can become capable of working on your navel and developing it. But you have no idea about it. You do not even know how much you are breathing or how little you are breathing – or how much is necessary. The more worried you become, the more you become filled with thoughts. You may be unaware that the more loaded the mind becomes the less the breathing will flow; it becomes obstructed.

Have you ever observed that breathing moves in one way when you are angry, and in a different way when you are peaceful? Have you ever observed that if there is an intense sexual desire in the mind the breathing moves in a particular way, but if the mind is filled with beautiful feelings then the breathing moves in a different way? Have you ever observed that a sick person's breathing moves in a particular way and a healthy person's breathing moves in a different way? The flow of the breath changes moment to moment, according to the state of your mind.

The contrary is also true: if the flow of your breath is absolutely harmonious, it changes the state of your mind. Either you change the mind and the breath changes, or you change the breath and it affects the mind.

For the person who wants to develop and influence his life centers, the first thing is rhythmic breathing. While sitting, standing or moving, his breath should be so harmonious, so peaceful, so deep that he should be able to experience a different music, a different harmony of the breath day and night. If you are walking on the road not doing any work, you will feel very blissful. If you breathe deeply, silently, slowly and harmoniously there will be two benefits. As long as breathing remains harmonious your thinking will become less, there will be almost no thoughts. If the breathing is absolutely even the thoughts in the mind will totally disappear.

The breathing affects the thoughts in the mind very deeply and to a very great extent. It costs nothing to breathe properly, and you do not have to spend any extra time to breathe properly. Sitting in a train, walking on the road, sitting at home, if the process of breathing deeply and peacefully continues then within a few days this process will become spontaneous. You will not even be aware of it: the breath will move deeply and slowly by itself.

The deeper and slower the flow of breath, the more your navel center will develop. Every time you breathe, the breath hits the navel center. If the breath goes in and out from above the navel center, then slowly the center becomes idle, it becomes weak because the breath does not hit it.

In the old days people found some clues, a formula for breathing. But man is so unintelligent that he starts repeating the formulas without seeing their meaning, without even understanding them. It is just like scientists finding a formula for water, H_2O. They say that with the combination of both hydrogen and oxygen water is created. Two atoms of hydrogen and one atom of oxygen make the formula H_2O. Now if a person starts repeating "H_2O, H_2O" in the same way as people are repeating "Ram, Ram, *aum*, *aum*", we will say he is mad – because what can happen by repeating a formula? The formula is only an indication of something. If you understand what it is about, then the formula is significant.

You can often hear people sitting and repeating the

sound of aum. They do not know that aum is a formula like H_2O. There are three letters in aum. They are 'a', 'u', 'm'. Perhaps you may not have noticed that if you close your mouth and say 'aa' loudly inside, you will feel the sound of 'a' resounding in your head. 'A' is an indication of the head center. If you say 'u' inside, then you will feel the sound of 'u' resounding within your heart. 'U' is an indication of the heart. And if you say 'm' inside, the third part of aum, then you will feel it resounding near your navel. 'A', 'u' and 'm' are three sounds indicating the sounds of the head, the heart and the navel. If you say 'm' you will feel the whole force of it on the navel. If you say 'u', you will feel the force going to the heart. If you say 'a', then 'a' will resound in the head and disappear.

This is a formula. One has to go from 'a' to 'u', and from 'u' to 'm'. Nothing will happen by just repeating aum. So those processes which take us in this direction – from 'a' to 'u' and from 'u' to 'm' – are the ones one must pay attention to. Deep breathing is the first process. The deeper the breath, the more harmonious, the more in tune it becomes, the more the life-energy within you will start arising, will start radiating from your navel. Your navel will become an alive center.

Within a few days you will start feeling that there is energy flowing out from your navel and you will also feel that there is energy coming in. You will find that a very living, a dynamic center is starting to develop near your navel. As soon as you feel this, many more experiences will start happening around this center.

Physiologically, breath is the first thing to develop the navel center. Psychologically, certain qualities are helpful to develop the navel. I told you in the morning about fearlessness. The more fearful a man is, the less close he will be able to reach to the navel center. The more fearless a man is, the closer he will reach to the navel.

So in educating children it is my essential suggestion that one should never tell a child, even by mistake, that he shouldn't go outside because it is dark. You are not aware that you are harming his navel center forever. Certainly, tell the children to go wherever there is darkness; tell them that the darkness is calling them. If the river is flooded, don't tell the children not to jump into it – because you do not know that the child who dares to enter a flooded river is developing his navel center. The navel center of a child who does not jump into the river becomes weak and feeble. If children want to climb mountains then let them. If children want to climb trees, let them. Let them go wherever they can experience adventure and fearlessness. Even if some children die each year climbing mountains, jumping into rivers or climbing trees, it does not matter at all. Because if all the children of a community become filled with fear and become lacking in fearlessness, then although the whole community may seem to be alive, it is actually dead.

In India this misfortune has happened. We talk a lot about religion but we know nothing about courage. We do not know that without courage there is no religion whatsoever, because without courage the central element of life remains undeveloped. One needs courage – so much courage that one is able to stand and face death. In India there is so much talk about religion but our fear of death has no limit! Actually, the contrary should be the case – people who know the soul, who recognize the soul should not be afraid of death at all because death does not exist. But while you talk a lot about the soul you are very afraid of death, immensely afraid.

Perhaps you talk about the soul because you are afraid of death. By talking about the soul you get some consolation that you will not die, that the soul is immortal. Perhaps you talk because of this fear – this seems to be the reality. Fearlessness should be developed. Immense fearlessness should be developed. So whenever there are opportunities in life to face danger, they should be welcomed.

Somebody once asked Nietzsche, "How can one develop one's personality?"

He gave a very peculiar maxim, one which you could not have expected. He said, "Live dangerously! Live dangerously if you want to develop your personality."

But you think that the more you live in security the better off you will be – there is a bank balance, a house, the police and the military are there, there is no fear.... You can have a quiet life in all this. You do not realize that in making these arrangements and these comforts, you have almost become dead. There is no point in living anymore because the only meaning in life is to live dangerously. There is no other meaning in living. Corpses are absolutely secure because now they cannot even die. Now nobody can kill them – their graves are absolutely safe.

An emperor built a palace. Because of security he made only one door to the palace. The neighboring emperor came to see it. He liked it very much and he said, "I would also like to build a similar palace. This is very secure. No enemy can enter it" – there was only one door, and there were great security arrangements at the door.

When the emperor departed the host emperor gave him a send-off and a big crowd gathered. While departing the emperor said, "This has made me very happy. I will also make such a palace."

There was an old man standing near him and he started laughing. The emperor asked, "Why are you laughing?"

The old man said, "If you make such a palace then don't make the mistake that he has made!"

"What mistake?" asked the emperor.

"Don't make even one door. Close all the doors. Then you will be absolutely safe," replied the old man.

The emperor said, "Then it will become a grave."

The old man said, "This palace has also become a grave. Wherever there is only one door and all kinds of security, and there is no danger from anywhere, it is a grave."

You think that the absence of fear is fearlessness: this

is a mistake. Fearlessness is not the absence of fear. In the presence of fear, fearlessness is a totally different thing which happens within. It is not the absence of fear. Fearlessness is the total presence of fear – with the courage to face it. But your lives are such that this does not develop.

My suggestion to you is this: by praying in the temples you will not reach closer to the divine. But when the adventures of life and fearlessness are inviting you, when dangers are calling you, if you go, you will certainly reach closer to the divine. In danger, in insecurity, the center which is hidden within you, which is sleeping, awakens and becomes alert. In danger, in insecurity, the center feels a challenge – and in this situation the navel center can develop.

In the old days, sannyasins accepted this insecurity. They left the home, but not because the home was wrong. Later, stupid people started thinking that sannyasins left the home because it was wrong, that they left their wives and children because they were a bondage. This idea is wrong. The sannyasin simply wanted to drop security. He wanted to enter the state of insecurity where there was no support, no friends, no acquaintances, no one to be called one's own. Wherever there might be sickness, death, dangers, poverty, he wanted to enter this state of insecurity. So someone who chose insecurity was a sannyasin.

But later on sannyasins created a great security for themselves, more than the people living in society! A person living in society has to earn his living, but a sannyasin does not: he is even more secure. He simply receives it – he gets clothes, he gets a place to live, he does not have to do without anything. The only difference is that he does not even have to earn it. The difficulty and insecurity of earning money is also finished. Someone else manages it for him, someone or other makes the arrangements for him. So a sannyasin becomes like a person tied to a peg, and this is why a sannyasin cannot be courageous. A sannyasin seems to be a person without any strength in this world; he cannot show even a little courage.

One sannyasin says, "I am a Jaina"; one sannyasin says, "I am a Hindu"; another sannyasin says, "I am a Mohammedan." Can a sannyasin be a Hindu, a Jaina or a Mohammedan? A sannyasin belongs to everybody. But there is a fear in saying, "I belong to everybody" – because to say that may mean that the sannyasin belongs to nobody. Then those who give him food, who make houses for him may no longer be friendly to him. They will say, "You do not belong to us. You belong to everybody so you can go to everybody. We will make arrangements for you only if you are Jaina monk," or "We will make arrangements for you if you are a Mohammedan monk. We are Mohammedans, so we will make arrangements only for Mohammedan monks." So the monk will say, "I am a Mohammedan," or he will say, "I am a Hindu." This is a search for security. This is a search for a new house: they have left the old house and now they want a new house.

So these days, the situation is such that those who

are clever, who want a good house, do not make a house at all – they simply become sannyasins! They say to others, "You are not wise – you make your own house. You commit sins and maybe you will go to hell!" And they get these people to build a house for them, they live in it, they enjoy the thoughts of going to heaven, they earn virtue and they escape from all the troubles of life. So sannyasins have created a security of their own.

But basically the meaning of sannyas is a longing to live in danger. Basically it means that there is no shelter, no companion, no certainty about tomorrow.

Christ was walking past a garden. He said to his friends, "Do you see these flowers which have blossomed in the garden? They do not know whether the sun will rise tomorrow or not. They do not know whether they will get water tomorrow or not – but today they have blossomed in their joy."

Man alone makes arrangements today for tomorrow, and then he makes arrangements for the day after tomorrow. There are people who make arrangements for how their grave should be built. Those who think they are wise create memorials beforehand in which to keep their dead bodies.

You all make arrangements and you completely forget that when a person makes arrangements for tomorrow, he kills today while making those arrangements. Then tomorrow he will again make arrangements for the next day, and he will kill that day also. Every day he will make arrangements for the following day and he will go on killing the present day. And there is nothing else but the present day. Tomorrow never comes: whenever it comes it is today. He kills today for tomorrow.

This is the nature of a mind looking for security: it kills today for tomorrow. It sacrifices the present for the future. And the future never comes. Tomorrow never comes. In the end he finds that his whole life has slipped out of his hands.

The person who dares to live today and does not even bother about tomorrow is living in danger – because tomorrow there may be danger. There is no certainty about anything. It is possible that the wife who is loving today may not be loving tomorrow; the husband who is loving today may not be loving tomorrow. There is no certainty about tomorrow. Today there is money, tomorrow there may be no money; today there are clothes, tomorrow there may be no clothes. In the person who totally accepts this insecurity about tomorrow and waits for tomorrow, faces whatever tomorrow brings, a center starts developing which I call the navel center. Within him a power, an energy, a potency arises. Within him a base arises, like a pillar of courage on which his life can grow.

So on the physical level breathing is needed, and on the psychological level courage is needed. These two things are basically necessary for the development of the navel center. If there is something else, or if you have some questions in your mind relating to this, I will talk to you about it tonight. But first, before this present session is over, I must tell you one more thing.

Seven or eight hundred years ago in Japan they tried to create a different type of person: they called him a samurai. He was a monk and also a warrior. This is very strange – what is the relation between a monk and a warrior? The temples in Japan are very strange. In these temples where they teach meditation they also teach jujitsu and judo and the arts of wrestling, swordsmanship and archery. If we were to go there and see, we would be surprised! What is the need to use a sword in a temple of meditation? And teaching judo, jujitsu and wrestling – how do they relate to meditation? In front of meditation temples there are symbols of swords. It is a very strange affair.

But there was a reason for it: meditators in Japan slowly came to realize that if there is no possibility in a seeker's life to develop courage and strength, then in that seeker only the mind will exist: his other deeper centers do not develop. He can only become a scholar, he cannot become a saint. He can become a so-called knowledgeable person. He can know the Gita, the Koran, the Bible and the Upanishads; he can memorize them like a parrot, this is possible – but he has no experience of life. So a meditator was taught how to use a sword and a bow and arrow.

Recently one of my friends returned from Japan. Someone there had given him a statue and he was very much troubled by it, he could not understand what kind of statue it was. When he returned he came to me with the statue and said, "Somebody has presented me with this statue, so I have brought it here because I have been wondering again and again what kind of a statue it is. What is its meaning?" It was a statue of a samurai warrior.

I told him, "You cannot understand because for thousands of years we have been creating a misunderstanding."

The statue was of a warrior with a naked sword in his hand. The side of the face which was on the same side as the hand with the sword was shining with the reflection of the sword. His face on that side looked like Arjuna's face might have done. In his other hand there was a lamp, and the light of the lamp was falling on the other side of his face: his face on that side looked like a face that Buddha, Mahavira or Christ might have had. There was a sword in one hand and a lamp in the other hand. You cannot understand it because you think that he should have either a sword or a lamp in his hand. How can both of these things be in the hands of one man?

So my friend was not able to understand it. He said to me, "I am very much puzzled. What is it all about?"

I told him that the lamp can only be in the hand of a person who also has a shining sword in his other hand. For him, it is not a question of *using* the sword; only weak people, fearful people use a sword. A person whose whole life becomes like a sword does not need to use it – there is no need for him to use it because his whole life is a sword.

So do not think that because a person has a sword

in his hands he will use it, that he will hurt or kill somebody. A person only kills when he is afraid of being killed himself – otherwise he will never kill. A violent person is really only a fearful person. In reality, a sword can only be held in the hands of a non-violent person. In fact, a person can only be non-violent when he himself becomes a sword, otherwise not.

The lamp of peace will only be of benefit to a man in whose being a sword of courage has been born, in whose being a sword of energy and strength has been born.

So on the one hand, the personality should be filled with total strength and on the other hand, with total peace: only then an integrated personality, a wholeness can arise.

Up to now there have been two kinds of situations in the world. People have either held lamps in their hands and become absolutely weak – if somebody blew out their lamp they could not even stop him or ask why he was blowing out the lamp. They would simply think that, "When this fellow goes away then we will light the lamp again, and if he does not go away then we will remain in darkness – either way there is no problem, so why take the trouble to resist?" So on the one hand, in one situation there are people who have a lamp in their hands but have no strength to protect it.

India has become one such weak country. It has become a weak country because we did not develop the real centers of our life-energy. We simply stayed with the mind, memorizing the Gita, the Upanishads and the sayings of Mahavira and went on making commentaries on them. The master and disciple went on sitting and talking about thousands of useless things which have no concern with life. Our whole country, our whole race has become weak, without any strength. It has become impotent.

And on the other hand, there are people who simply stopped caring about the lamp, who took up the sword and started using it. Then, because they did not have a lamp, they could not see in the darkness who they were killing. They did not know whether they were killing their own people or others. So they just went on killing, and if someone started talking about lighting the lamp they said, "Stop talking nonsense. The time spent in lighting the lamp can be spent in using the sword. And also, one more sword can be made with the metal with which we would make the lamp, so why waste all that oil and all that metal? Life is all about using the sword."

People in the West are using their swords in darkness and people in the East are sitting there with a lamp but with no sword. And both are crying. The whole world is crying. A right man has not been created: the right man is both a living sword and a lamp of peace. I call somebody a religious man only if both of these things have arisen in him.

Today we have talked on these first points. It is good if many questions about this arise in your minds; they should arise. If you write down those questions then I can answer you tonight. Then tomorrow, we will begin to discuss some other points. So today, ask questions only about what we have discussed today and not about anything else. Tomorrow we will talk about these other points and then you can ask questions about them. The day after tomorrow we will talk about more points and then you can ask questions about them. But today it will be better if you ask questions about whatever I have just talked about. If you have any questions which are not concerned with the talks of these three days, you can ask them on the last day and we can talk about them then.

THE NAVEL, SEAT OF WILL

CHAPTER THREE

THE NAVEL: SEAT OF WILL

My beloved ones,

How can the life of man become centered in his being, how can he experience himself, how can he attain his own self? – we have discussed this in the previous two talks of today. Some more things have been asked. In answer to them I will talk to you now on three points. Tomorrow and the day after tomorrow I will answer the questions which are not related to today's discussion.

And now I will answer the questions which are related to today's discussion, dividing them into three points.

The first point is about how a man should start living his life from the navel center, centered in the self, centered in his being. Before I go into this I would like to discuss three other significant ways through which the energy that is dormant in the navel can become awake. Once it is awake, it becomes a door through which man can experience a consciousness which is different from his body. I will tell you the three points, then I will discuss them.

The first point is right-diet, the second point is right-work and the third point is right-sleep. A person who does not get a right-diet, right-work and right-sleep can never become centered at the navel. Man has lost touch with all these three things.

Man is the only species whose diet is not predictable. The diet of all other animals is certain. Their basic physical needs and their nature decides what they should eat and what they should not, how much they should eat and how much they should not, when they should eat and when they should stop. But man is absolutely unpredictable, he is absolutely uncertain: neither does his nature tell him what he should eat nor his awareness tell him how much he should eat nor does his understanding decide when he should stop eating. As none of these qualities of man are predictable, the life of man has gone in some very uncertain directions. But if there is even a little understanding, if man starts living with even a little intelligence, with even a little thoughtfulness, opening his eyes even a little, then it is not at all difficult to change to a right-diet. It is very easy; nothing can be more easy. To understand right-diet we can divide it into two parts.

The first thing: what should a man eat and what should he not eat? Man's body is made of chemical elements; the whole process of the body is very much chemical. If alcohol is put into a man, then his body will be affected by the chemical: it will become intoxicated, unconscious. Howsoever healthy, howsoever peaceful the man may be, the chemistry of the intoxicant will affect his body. Howsoever saintly a man may be, if he is given poison then he will die.

Socrates died from poisoning and Gandhi died from a bullet. A bullet does not see whether the man is a saint or a sinner; neither does poison see whether the man is Socrates or some ordinary person. Neither do the harmful intoxicants and poisons nor does the food see who or what you are. Their functions are straightforward – they go into the chemistry of the body and start working. In this way, any food which is intoxicating will start harming and creating disturbances in man's consciousness. Any food which takes man into any kind of unconsciousness, any kind of excitement, any kind of extremity, any kind of disturbance, is harmful. And the deepest, ultimate harm is when these things start reaching the navel.

Perhaps you are not aware that in naturopathy, all over the world, mud packs, vegetarian food, light food, water-soaked cloth strips and tub baths are used to heal the body. But no naturopath has yet understood the point that the effects on the body of water-soaked cloth strips, mud packs or tub baths are not so much because of their special qualities but because of how they affect the navel center. And the navel center then affects the rest of the body. All these things – the mud, the water, the tub bath – affect the dormant energy in the navel center, and when this energy arises the person starts to become healthy.

But naturopathy is still not aware of this. Naturopathy thinks that perhaps these beneficial effects are coming from the mud packs, the tub baths or the wet strips on the stomach! They do have benefits, but the real benefits are coming from the awakening of energy in the dormant navel center.

If the navel center is mistreated, if a wrong diet, wrong food is used, then slowly, slowly the navel center will become dormant and its energy will become weaker. Slowly, slowly that center will start falling asleep. Finally, it will almost go to sleep. Then we are not even aware of it as a center. Then we are aware of only two centers: one is the mind where thoughts are constantly moving, and the other is a little bit of the heart where emotions are moving. We have no contact with anything deeper than this. So the lighter the food is, the less it creates heaviness on the body, the more valuable and significant it will be for the beginning of your inner journey.

For a right-diet, the first thing to remember is that it should not create excitement, it should not be intoxicating, it should not be heavy. After eating rightly you should not feel heaviness and drowsiness. But perhaps all of us feel heaviness and drowsiness after our meals: then we should know that we are eating wrongly.

A very great doctor, Kenneth Walker, has said in his autobiography that, according to his lifelong experiences, whatever people eat, half of it fills their stomachs and half of it fills the stomachs of the doctors. If they were to eat only half of what they usually eat, they would not become sick at all and there would be no need for any doctors.

Some people get sick because they do not get enough food, and some people get sick because they get too much food. Some people die of hunger and some people die of overeating. And the number of people dying of overeating has always been more than the people dying of hunger. Very few people die of hunger. Even if a man wants to starve himself, there is no possibility of his dying for at least three months. Anyone can live without food for three months. But if a man overeats for three months, then there is no possibility that he will survive.

There have been people whose very ideas make us feel strange. There was a great emperor called Nero. He had two doctors whose job it was just to make him vomit after his meals so that he could enjoy eating at least fifteen to twenty times a day. He would eat a meal and then he would take medicine to make him vomit so that he could enjoy food again. But what we are doing is not very different.

Nero could have doctors at his palace because he was an emperor. We are not emperors, but we have doctors in our neighborhoods. Nero was making himself vomit every day, we make ourselves vomit every few months. We eat a wrong diet and accumulate all kinds of things. Then the doctor gives us a cleansing and we start eating the wrong food again. Nero was a wise man – he arranged for a cleansing every day. We do it only after every two or three months. If we were also emperors then we would do the same thing, but we are helpless – we do not have the facilities so we cannot do it. We laugh at Nero, but in a certain way we are not different from him.

Our wrong attitudes towards food are becoming dangerous to us. They are proving to be very costly. They have taken us to a point where we are somehow barely alive. Our food does not seem to create health in us, it seems to create sickness. It is a surprising situation when our food starts making us sick. It is as if

the sunrise in the morning were to create darkness –
this would be an equally surprising and strange thing
to happen. But all the physicians in the world are of
the opinion that most of the diseases of man are because of his wrong diet.

So the first thing is that every person should be very
aware and conscious about his eating. And I am saying
this especially for the meditator. It is necessary for a
meditator to remain aware of what he eats, how much
he eats and what its effects are on his body. If you experiment for a few months with awareness, you will
certainly find out which is the right food for you, which
food gives you tranquility, peace and health. There are
no real difficulties, but because you do not pay any attention to your food you are never able to discover the
right food.

The second thing about food is that the state of your
mind when you eat is much more important than what
you eat. Food will affect you differently if you eat joyously, happily or if you eat when you are filled with
sadness and worry.

If you are eating in a worried state, then even the
best food will have a poisonous effect. And if you are
eating with joy, then it is possible that sometimes even
poison may not be able to have its total effect on you –
it is very possible. So the state of mind you are in when
you eat is important.

In Russia there was a great psychologist called
Pavlov. He did some experiments on animals and
reached an amazing conclusion. He experimented

on both cats and dogs. He gave food to a cat and he observed the cat through an X-ray machine to see what happened in her stomach after she ate her food. When the food went into the stomach, the stomach immediately released digestive juices. At the same time a dog was brought to the window of the room that the cat was in. When the dog barked the cat became afraid, and the X-ray machine showed that the secretion of digestive juices within her had stopped. The stomach closed; it shrank. Then the dog was taken away, but for six hours her stomach remained in the same condition. The digestive process of the food did not begin again and the food remained undigested in the stomach for six hours. After six hours, when the juices started flowing again, the food was not in a digestible state: it had become solid and difficult to digest. When the cat's mind became worried about the presence of the dog the stomach stopped its work.

Then what about your situation? – you live in worry for twenty-four hours a day. It is a miracle how the food you eat is digested, how existence manages it in spite of you! You have no wish to digest it. It is an absolute miracle how it is digested. And how you remain alive is also a miracle! Your state of mind should be graceful and blissful.

But in your houses, the dining table is in the most gloomy state. The wife waits the whole day for her husband to come home to eat and all the emotional sickness she has gathered in the last twenty-four hours comes out just when the husband is eating. She does not know that she is doing the work of an enemy. She does not know that she is serving poison on her husband's plate.

The husband is also afraid and worried after the whole day's work – he somehow dumps the food into his stomach and leaves. He has no idea that this act which he has finished so quickly and has run away from should have been a prayerful one. It was not an act which should have been done in a hurry. It should have been done in the same way as someone entering a temple, as someone kneeling to pray, as someone sitting to play his *veena* or as someone singing a song for the beloved. This act is even more important: he is giving food to his body. It should be done in a state of tremendous blissfulness; it should be a loving and prayerful act.

The more happily and joyously and the more relaxed and without worry a person can be when eating, the more his food will start becoming the right food.

A violent diet does not mean only that a man eats nonvegetarian food: it is also a violent diet when a man eats with anger. Both of these things are violent. While eating in anger, in suffering, in worry, man is also eating violently. He does not realize at all that just as he is violent when eating the flesh of something, so is it when his own flesh burns up inside because of anger and worry; then violence is present there too. Then the food which he is eating cannot be nonviolent.

The other part of right-food is that you should eat in a very peaceful, a very joyful state. If you are not in such a state, then it is better to wait until you are and not to eat for a while. When the mind is absolutely ready, only then should you eat your meals. How long will it take for the mind to be ready? If you are aware enough to wait, then at the most it can remain disturbed for only a day. But you have never bothered to listen to it; you have made eating food a completely mechanical process. You put food into the body and then leave the dining table – it is no longer a psychological process, and that is dangerous.

On the body level, right-food should be healthy, non-stimulating and nonviolent; on the psychological level the mind should be in a blissful state, graceful and joyous; and on the level of the soul there should be a feeling of gratefulness, of thankfulness. These three things make food the right-food.

You should have a feeling that, "Because food is available to me today, I am grateful. I have been given one more day to live and I am tremendously grateful. This morning I have woken up alive again; today the sun has given its light to me again; today I will be able to see the moon again; I am alive again today! It was not necessary that I should have been alive today, today I could have been in my grave – but life has again been given to me. I have not earned it, it has been given to me for nothing." For this at least, a feeling of thankfulness, of gratitude should be there in your heart. You are eating food, you are drinking water, you are breathing – you should have a sense of gratefulness for all this. Towards all of life, towards the whole world, towards the whole universe, towards all of nature, towards the divine, there should be a feeling of gratefulness: "I have received one more day to live. Once more I have received food to eat. For one more day I am seeing the sun, seeing the flowers blossoming. I am alive again today."

Two days before death came to Rabindranath he said, "Lord, how grateful I am! Oh God, how shall I express my gratitude? You gave this life to me when I was not in any way worthy of receiving it. You gave breathing to me when I had no right to breathe. You gave me experiences of beauty and bliss which I had not earned at all. I am grateful. I am overwhelmed by your grace. And if in this life that you have given I may have received any pain, any suffering, any worry, it must have been my fault, because this life of yours is very blissful. It must have been my fault. So I do not ask you to give me liberation from life. If you feel me worthy, then send me into this life again and again. This life of yours is very blissful and I am utterly grateful for it."

This feeling, this feeling of gratitude should be present in all aspects of life – and very particularly concerning your diet. Only then can your diet become the right-diet.

The second point is: right-work. That too is no longer an essential part of your life. Physical work has become a shameful act.

A Western thinker, Albert Camus, has jokingly written in one of his letters that a time will come when people will start asking their servants to make love for them. If someone falls in love with somebody, he will appoint a servant to go and make love on his behalf. This may happen some day! You have already started having everything done by others; making love is the only thing which you still do yourselves. You appoint others to pray for you. You employ a priest and tell him to pray on your behalf, to do the rituals on your behalf. You appoint a priest in the temple and tell him to worship on your behalf. You are even having your servants do things like prayer and worship. So if you are getting your servants to worship for you, it is not unthinkable that some day wise people will tell their servants to make love to their beloved on their behalf. What is the difficulty? And those who will not be able to afford servants to do the job will feel ashamed that they are so poor, that they have to make love themselves.

It is possible some day, because there is so much in life which is significant but which you are now getting done by your servants! And you are not at all aware of what you have lost by losing the significant things. All the strength, all the vitality of life is lost because man's body and man's being have been created for a certain amount of work – and now he has been spared all that work.

Right-work is also an essential part in the awakening of man's consciousness and energy.

One morning, Abraham Lincoln was polishing his

shoes in his house. One of his friends who was visiting him said, "Lincoln! What are you doing? You polish your own shoes?"

Lincoln said, "You surprise me! Do you polish other people's shoes? I am polishing my own shoes – do you polish others' shoes?"

The friend said, "No, no, I get my shoes polished by others!"

Lincoln said, "It is even worse to get your shoes polished by others than to polish others' shoes."

What does it mean? It means that we are losing our direct contact with life. Our direct contacts with life are those that come through work.

Once, when Confucius was alive about three thousand years ago, he went to visit a village. In a garden he saw an old gardener and his son pulling water out of a well. For the old man, the work of drawing water out of a well was very difficult even with the help of his son. And the old man was *very* old.

Confucius wondered if this old man did not know that bullocks and horses were now being used to draw water out of a well; he was drawing it himself. He was using such old methods!

So Confucius went to the old man and said, "My friend! Don't you know that there has been a new invention? People are drawing water out of wells with the help of horses and bullocks. Why are you doing it yourself?"

The old man said, "Speak softly, speak softly. For me, it does not matter what you say, but I am afraid my young son may hear you."

Confucius asked, "What do you mean?"

The old man replied, "I know about these inventions, but all inventions like this take man away from physical work. I do not want my son to become disconnected, because the day he becomes disconnected from physical work he will be disconnected from life itself."

Life and work are synonymous. Life and work have the same meaning. But slowly, slowly you have started calling those people who do not have to do physical work fortunate and those who have to do physical work unfortunate. And in a way it has become like this, because in a way many people have dropped working, so some people have to do too much work. Too much work kills you, too little work also kills you. Hence I say right-work, the proper distribution of physical work. Each person should do some physical work. The more intensely, the more blissfully, the more gratefully a man enters the work part of his life, the more he will find that his life-energy has started moving down from the brain and closer to the navel. For work, neither the brain nor the heart are needed. The energy for work is derived directly from the navel, this is its source.

Along with the right-diet, a little physical work is absolutely essential. And it is not that it should be in the interests of others – that if you serve the poor it benefits the poor; that if you go to a village and do farming it benefits the farmers; that if you are doing some labor you are doing a great social service. These are all false things. It is for your own sake, not for anyone else's sake. It is not concerned with benefiting anybody else. Someone else may benefit by it, but primarily it is for your own good.

When Churchill retired, one of my friends went to see him at his house. In his old age, Churchill was digging and planting some plants in his garden. My friend asked him some questions about politics. Churchill said, "Drop it! Now it is over. Now if you want to ask me something, you can ask me about two things. You can ask me about the Bible because I read it at home, and you can ask me about gardening because I do it here in the garden. I have no interest in politics now. That time is over. Now I am simply working and praying."

When my friend returned he said to me, "I do not understand what kind of man Churchill is. I thought he would give me some answers, but he said he was simply working and praying."

I told him, "To say working *and* praying is a repetition. Work and prayer mean the same thing, they are synonymous. And the day that work becomes prayer and prayer becomes work is the day that right-work will be attained."

A little physical labor is absolutely essential, but you have not paid any attention to it. Not even the traditional sannyasins of India have paid any attention to work:

they have refrained from doing it, there was no question of their doing it. They simply moved in another direction. Rich people stopped physical work because they had the money and they could pay someone else to do it, and sannyasins stopped because they had nothing more to do with the world. They did not have to create anything or to earn money, so what did they need work for? The result was that two respected classes of society moved away from work. So the people in whose hands working remained slowly, slowly became disrespected.

For a seeker, physical work has great significance and usefulness – not because you will produce something out of it but because the more you are involved in some kind of work, the more your consciousness will start becoming centered, it will start coming downwards from the mind. It is not necessary for the work to be productive. It can be nonproductive also, it can be a simple exercise. But some physical labor is absolutely essential for the agility of the body, the complete alertness of the mind and the total awakening of the being. This is the second part.

But one can make mistakes in this part also. Just as one can make a mistake with one's diet – eating either too little or too much – so a mistake can happen here also: one can either do no physical exercise at all or do too much. Wrestlers do too much exercise: they are in a sick state. A wrestler is not a healthy person. A wrestler is putting too much of a burden on the body, he is raping the body. If the body is raped then some parts of the body, some muscles, can become more developed – but no wrestler lives long! No wrestler dies in a healthy state. Do you know that all wrestlers – whether he is a Gama, a Sandow or anybody else with a great body, even the greatest in the world – die un- healthy? They die prematurely, and they die of violent diseases. Raping the body can develop the muscles and make the body worth looking at, worth exhibiting, but there is a great difference between exhibition and life. There is a great difference between living, being healthy, and being an exhibitionist.

Each person should find out according to himself, according to his body, how much physical work he should do to live more healthily and more freshly. The more fresh air there is inside the body, the more bliss- ful each and every breath is, the more vitality a person will have to explore the inner. Simone Weil, a French philosopher, has written a very wonderful thing in her autobiography. She said, "Until the age of thirty I was always sick. I was unhealthy and I had many head- aches. But it was only at the age of forty that I realized that until the age of thirty I had been a materialist. I became healthy when I became more spiritual. It was only later that I saw that my being sick and unhealthy was related to my materialism."

A person who is sick and unhealthy cannot be full of gratitude towards existence. There can be no thankful- ness in him towards existence: there is only anger. It is impossible for such a person to accept something from existence when he is full of anger towards it. He simply rejects it. If one's life does not attain a certain balance of health through right-work and right-exercise, then it is natural that one will feel some negativity, a resistance, an anger towards life.

Right-work is an essential rung on the ladder to ultimate religiousness.

The third point is right-sleep. Eating has become disrupted, physical work has become disrupted – and sleep has been totally murdered! The thing which has been harmed the most in the development of human civilization is sleep. From the day man discovered artificial light, his sleep has become very troubled. And as more and more gadgets started coming into his hands, he started feeling sleep to be an unnecessary thing, too much time is wasted in it: the time when we are asleep is completely wasted. So the less sleep he could do with, the better. It does not occur to people that sleep has any kind of contribution to the deeper processes of life. Some people think that the time spent sleeping is time wasted, so the less they sleep the better; the more quickly they reduce the amount of sleep, the better.

This is one type of person, wanting to reduce the amount of sleep needed. Another type has been the monks and the hermits who felt that this sleep, this unconsciousness in the form of sleep, was the opposite to the state of self-realization or self-awakening. So according to them it was not good to sleep, and the less you slept the better.

There was one more problem for the monks: they had

collected too many repressions in their unconscious, and in sleep all that repression started surfacing and entering their dreams. So a kind of fear of sleep arose, because all the things that they had ignored during the day started surfacing in their sleep at night. The women they had left and run away from into the forest started appearing in their sleep. These monks started seeing them in their dreams. The money and the prestige that the monks had run away from started following them in their dreams. So they felt that sleep was a very dangerous thing – out of their control – so the less they slept the better. These monks created a kind of feeling in the whole world that sleep is something unspiritual. This is an extremely foolish notion.

So the first group of people oppose sleep and feel that it is a waste of time, that there is no need to sleep for so long – the more time a person remains awake the better.

People who calculate everything and make statistics about everything are really strange. They have calculated that if a person sleeps for eight hours, one-third of his day goes in sleeping. If a person lives for sixty years, then twenty years have gone to waste. Out of a lifespan of sixty years, only forty years are available for use. And then they have calculated even further: they have calculated how much time a man takes to eat, to put on his clothes, shave, bathe and so on. After calculating everything they stated that almost our whole lives go to waste. When they started subtracting all that time, they realized that a person only appears to live for sixty years: in reality twenty years go in sleep, some years go in eating, some years go in bathing, some years go in reading the newspaper. Everything goes to waste and nothing remains of life. These people created a panic – their advice was to cut down on all these things if you want to have some time to live. Sleep takes up the most time in a man's life, so reduce it. So, while this group were advising a reduction in sleep and creating a wave of opposition to sleep, the second group, the monks and hermits, were calling sleep unspiritual and telling people to sleep as little as possible. The less a person slept the more of a saintly person he was – and if he did not sleep at all then he was a totally saintly person.

These two groups and their ideas have destroyed man's ability to sleep, and with the murder of sleep all the deep centers of man's life have been shaken, disturbed and become uprooted. We have not even noticed that the cause behind all the illnesses, all the disorders that have entered man's life is his lack of sleep.

The person who cannot sleep rightly cannot live rightly. Sleep is not a waste of time. The eight hours of sleep are not being wasted: rather, it is because of those eight hours that you are able to stay awake for sixteen hours. Otherwise you would not be able to stay awake all that time. During those eight hours life-energy is accumulated, your life is revitalized, the centers of your brain and heart calm down and your life functions from your navel center. For those eight hours of sleep you again become one with nature and with existence – that is why you become revitalized.

If you want to torture somebody then the best method – invented thousands of years ago – is to prevent him from going to sleep. It has not been possible to improve upon this method so far. During the last war in Germany, and even now in Russia, the most popular method of torturing prisoners is to prevent them from sleeping. You simply don't allow the person to sleep. This is torture beyond all limits for the person. So guards were put next to the prisoners to disturb their sleep.

The Chinese first discovered this method some two thousand years ago. Simply not allowing a person to sleep was a very cheap method of torture. They would make the man stand in a cell which was so small that he could not move at all, could neither sit nor lie down. Then they would drip water from above which would fall on his head, drop by drop. He could not move at all, neither sit nor lie down, so after twelve, sixteen or at the most eighteen hours he would start shouting and screaming, – "Help! I'm going to die! Get me out of here!" Then they would ask him to tell them the things he was concealing. And after three days even the most courageous person would give up.

Hitler in Germany and Stalin in Russia did the same thing with hundreds of thousands of people: they would keep them awake and not let them sleep. One cannot experience a worse torture than this. Even if you kill someone, he does not suffer as much as when you do not let him sleep – because it is only in sleeping that he regains what he has lost. If he is unable to sleep, then he goes on losing and losing his life-energy, without being able to regenerate. He becomes totally dried out. We are a dried-out humanity because our doors for receiving something are closed and our doors for losing everything have become more and more open.

Sleep needs to come back into man's life. Really, there is no alternative, no other step than that for the psychological health of humanity. Sleep should be made compulsory by law for the next one or two hundred years! It is very important for a meditator to see to it that he sleeps properly and enough.

And one more thing needs to be understood: right-sleep will be different for everybody. It will not be the same for everyone, because the body has needs which are different for each person according to age and to many other variables.

For example, when a child is in the mother's womb, he sleeps for twenty-four hours a day because all his tissues are developing. He needs complete sleep; his body will develop only if he keeps on sleeping for twenty-four hours a day. It is possible that children who are born lame or crippled or blind woke up during the nine months in their mother's womb. Perhaps some day science will realize that the children who somehow wake up in the mother's womb are born crippled, or with part of their body undeveloped.

It is necessary to remain asleep in the womb for twenty-four hours a day because the whole body is being created, the whole body is developing. A very deep sleep is necessary; only then can all the activities of the body take place. When a child is born he sleeps for twenty hours a day – his body is still growing. Then he sleeps for eighteen hours, then fourteen hours.... Slowly, slowly, as his body starts becoming mature, he also sleeps less and less. In the end it settles at a time between six and eight hours.

An old man sleeps less – it becomes five hours, four hours, even three hours – because the growth of the body of an old man has stopped. He does not need much sleep every day because now his death is coming close. If an old man were to sleep as much as a child sleeps, then he could not die, death would be difficult. Death needs less and less sleep. Life needs deep sleep. That is why an old man, by and by, starts sleeping less and less and a child sleeps more.

If old people start expecting the same behavior from children as they do from themselves, it will become dangerous.

And old people often do this: they treat children as if they were also old. They wake them up too early in the morning: 'It is three o'clock, it is four o'clock! Get up!' They are not aware that it is alright if they wake up at four o'clock because they are old. But children cannot wake up at four o'clock. To wake them up is wrong. It is harming the body functions of the child; it is very harmful for them.

A child once said to me, "My mother is very strange – when I am not feeling sleepy at all at night she forces me to sleep, and when I feel sleepy in the morning she forces me to wake up. I do not understand why I am forced to sleep when I am not sleepy and I am forced to wake up when I am sleepy. You explain things to many people, can't you explain this to my mother?" He wanted me to help his mother understand that what she was doing was very contradictory.

We are not aware that children are often treated like old people and then, as they grow older, they have to start living according to many fixed rules written in many books.

Perhaps you may not be aware that the latest research says that there cannot be one fixed time for everyone to wake up. It has always been said that it is good for everyone to wake up at five o'clock in the morning – this is absolutely wrong and unscientific. It is not good for everyone: it may be good for some people but it may be harmful for others. In twenty-four hours, for about three hours the body temperature of each person goes down, and those three hours are the hours of deepest sleep. If you wake the person up during those three hours his whole day will be spoiled and his whole energy will be disturbed.

Generally, these three hours are between two and five in the morning. For most people these three hours are from two to five in the morning, but it is not the case with everyone. For some people their body temperature is low until six o'clock, for some it is low until seven and for some their temperature starts becoming normal at four in the morning. So if someone wakes up within these hours of low temperature, all twenty-four hours of his day will be spoiled and there will be harmful effects. Only when a person's temperature starts rising to a normal level is it time for him to wake up.

Normally it is alright for everybody to wake up with the rising sun, because as the sun rises everyone's temperature starts rising. But this is not a rule, there are some exceptions. For some people it may be necessary to sleep a little later than sunrise, because each individual's body temperature rises at a different time, at a different pace. So each person should find out how many hours of sleep he needs and what is a healthy time for him to get up, and that is the rule for him. Whatever the scriptures may say, whatever the gurus may say, there is no need to listen to them at all.

For right-sleep, the deeper and the longer you are able to sleep, the better. But I am telling you to sleep, not to keep on lying on the bed. Lying down on your bed is not sleep.

To wake up when you feel it is healthy for you to wake up should be the rule for you. Usually it happens along with the sunrise, but it is possible that this does not happen to you. There is no need to be afraid or worried or to think that you are a sinner and be afraid of going to hell. Many people who get up early in the morning go to hell and many people who get up late are living in heaven! None of this has any relation whatsoever to being spiritual or unspiritual – but right-sleep certainly does have a relationship with it.

So each person should discover what is the best arrangement for him. For three months each person should experiment with his work, with his sleep and with his diet, and should find out what are the most healthy, most peaceful and most blissful rules for him.

And everyone should make his own rules. No two persons are alike, so no common rule is ever applicable to everybody. Whenever someone tries to apply a common rule, it has a bad effect. Each person is an individual. Each person is unique and incomparable. Only he is like himself, there is no other person like him anywhere on the earth. So no rule can be a rule for him until he finds out what the rules for his own life-processes are.

Books, scriptures and gurus are dangerous because they have readymade formulas. They tell you that you should wake up at a certain time, you should eat this, you should not eat that, you should sleep like this and you should do things in this way. These readymade formulas are dangerous. It is good to understand them, but each person has to make his own arrangements for his life.

Each person has to find his own path of meditation. Each person has to walk by himself and create a path for his spiritual journey. There is no readymade highway for you to go and start walking on; there is no such highway anywhere. The path of the spiritual journey is like a small footpath – but a footpath that is not even there! – you create it as you walk along it and it continues for howsoever long you walk on it. And the more you walk, the more your understanding of the journey that is yet to come will develop.

So these three points have to be kept in mind: right-diet, right-work and right-sleep. If life proceeds rightly on these three points, then there is more possibility of opening what I call the navel center – which is the door to spiritual life. If you get close to that door, it opens; then a very unique thing happens, something of which you have had no experience in your ordinary life.

Last evening, when I left here, a friend came and said, "What you say is alright, but until we have contentment, it is very difficult to be convinced." I did not say anything to him. Perhaps he thinks that he will get contentment by my talking about it – but he is absolutely wrong and is wasting his time. I make whatever effort is needed from my side, but an even greater effort must be made from your side. If you do not make the effort there is no purpose, no meaning in my saying anything.

People constantly say to me that they want peace, they want bliss, they want a soul. Yes, you want everything, but you do not get anything in the world just by wanting it. Desire alone is absolutely impotent, there is no strength in it.

Desire alone is not enough: determination and effort are also needed. It is alright that you desire something, but how much effort do you make for that desire, how many steps do you take towards that desire, what do you do for that desire?

According to my criterion, the only proof of your desire is the effort you make to satisfy it. Otherwise, there is no proof that you have a desire. When a person desires something he makes some effort to get it: that effort is the proof that the person desired something. You say that you desire, but you have no intention of making any effort to get it. You have no determination for it.

To close this talk I will repeat one more point. I told you about the three centers: the center of intellect is the mind, the center of feelings is the heart. What is the navel the center of? The navel is the center of will-power. The more activated the navel is, the more intense the willpower becomes and the more you can attain the determination, the power, the life-energy to do something.

Or think of it in reverse: the more determined you are, the more you gather energy for doing, the more your navel center will develop. Both of these are inter-dependent, related to each other; the more you think, the more your intellect will develop; the more you love, the more your heart will develop. The more determined you are, the more the center of your inner energy, that central lotus of the navel, will develop.

A small story, and then I will finish my talk.

A blind fakir was begging in a town and came to a mosque. He spread out his hands in front of the door of the mosque and asked, "Can I get something to eat? I am hungry."

The people passing by said, "Idiot! This is not a house where you can get something to eat. This is a mosque, a temple; nobody lives here. You are begging at a mosque – you will not get anything here. Go somewhere else."

The fakir laughed. He said, "If I do not get anything from the house of God, then from what other house can I get anything? This is the last house I have come to, and by mistake this last house is a temple. How can I move away from here? If I move, where will I go? There is no other house after this one, so now I will stay here and I will only move when I get something."

The people started laughing at him. They said, "Idiot! Nobody lives here. Who will give anything to you?"

He replied, "That is not the question. If I have to leave the house of God with empty hands, then where will my hands be filled? Then my hands will not be filled anywhere. Now that I have stumbled upon this door I will leave only when my hands are full."

And the fakir stayed there. For one year his hands remained spread out in the same way, and his being went on longing in the same way. The people of the town started saying he was mad. They said to him, "You are absolutely a fool! Where do you think you are sitting with your hands spread out? There is nothing to be gained here."

But the fakir was one of a kind, someone unique – he remained sitting and sitting and sitting.

After a year had passed by, the people of the town saw that perhaps the fakir had attained something: the aura around his face had changed. There was a kind of peaceful breeze floating around him; a kind of light appeared around him, a fragrance. The man started dancing. Where before there had been tears in his eyes, now there was a smile on his face. He had been almost dead, but in this one year his life blossomed again and he started dancing.

People asked, "Have you attained something?"

He said, "It would have been impossible not to gain something, because I had decided that I would either gain something or I would die. I have attained more than I desired. I desired only food for my body and I have gained food for my soul also. I wanted only to fulfill the hunger of my body, but now the hunger of my soul has also been fulfilled."

They started asking, "How did you attain this? How did you gain this?"

He said, "I *did* nothing, but I put all my willpower behind my thirst. I said to myself that if there is a thirst, then along with it there should also be a total determination. My total determination was behind my thirst, and now my thirst has been quenched. I have reached to the place where that water is available, and after drinking it my thirst has gone."

The meaning of determination is to have the courage, the inner strength and willpower to do something about whatever it is you want, to act according to whatever you think is right and to follow whichever path seems right to you. If you do not have this determination, then nothing can happen through my or anybody else's words. If something could happen through my words then things would be very easy. There have been many people in the world who have said very good things: if things could have happened just through their words, by now everything would have happened to the whole world. But neither Mahavira nor Buddha nor Christ nor Krishna nor Mohammed could do anything. Nobody can do anything unless you yourself are ready to do it.

The Ganges goes on flowing, the oceans are full – but you have no bucket in your hands and you are shouting that you want water.

The Ganges says, "There is water, but where is your container?" You say, "Don't talk about the container. You are the Ganges, there is so much water in you – give some to me."

The doors to the Ganges are not closed, the doors to the Ganges are open – but you need a container.

On the spiritual journey, where there is no container of determination, no fulfillment or contentment can ever be attained.

You have listened to my talks so silently....

The three meetings of our first day now come to an end, and from tomorrow we will start discussing the other two points. Now, after this meeting, we will sit for the night meditation for about ten minutes.

You should understand two or three things regarding the night meditation, then we will sit for it. Would it be possible to lie down? Is there space enough for the meditators to lie down? First understand, then we will do the night meditation. The morning meditation is to be done sitting. Life arises, wakes up in the morning, so it is helpful to meditate sitting up. The night meditation has to be done lying in bed, before you go to sleep. After the meditation just go to sleep silently: this is the last thing in the day. The morning meditation is the first thing that happens after waking up, the night meditation is the last thing that happens before going to sleep.

If one properly enters a state of meditation before sleeping, one's whole sleep is transformed. One's whole sleep can become a meditation because sleep has certain rules. The first rule is that the last thought at night will become the central thought in your sleep, and it will be your first thought on waking up in the morning. If you have gone to sleep at night in anger, then throughout the night your mind and your dreams will be filled with anger. And when you wake up in the morning you will find that your first feeling and your first thought will be of anger. Whatever we take to sleep with us at night stays with us the whole night.

That is why I say that if you need to carry something into your sleep, then it is better to carry meditation with you, so that the whole sleep revolves around meditation, around its peace. Slowly, slowly within a few days you will find that dreams disappear, that your sleep becomes like a deep river. And when you wake up in the morning from a deep sleep – deep from this night meditation – your first thoughts will be of peace, of bliss, of love. So the morning journey has to be started with the morning meditation and the night journey has to be started with the night meditation.

The night meditation has to be done while lying down, while lying down in bed. We will do the experiment here lying down.

And after you have laid down you have to do three things. The first thing is that the body has to be totally relaxed, as if there is no life in it – so loose, so relaxed, no life in the body. And for three minutes your mind has to feel that the body is becoming relaxed, more relaxed, more relaxed because whatever the mind feels the body will follow it. The body is just a servant, a follower. The body expresses whatever we feel through action. If you feel anger the body picks up a stone to throw; if you feel love the body hugs somebody. Whatever you want to be, whatever you want to do, when the thought arises in the mind the body turns it into action.

Every day we see the miracle of the body transforming a thought into action whenever it arises. We never think of becoming relaxed, otherwise the body would do that too. The body can relax so much that one does not even know if it exists or not – but that only happens after doing this experiment for a while. For three minutes you have to go on feeling relaxed.

Right now, I will give you suggestions so that you come to experience the feeling. When I give you the suggestion that the body is becoming relaxed, then you will feel that the body is becoming more relaxed, more relaxed.... The body will become relaxed.

As the body becomes relaxed, the breath will become calm. Calmness does not mean that breathing will stop but it will become slow, tranquil and deep. Then for three minutes you have to feel that your breathing is becoming calmer and calmer, the breathing is becoming relaxed.... Then slowly the mind also will become relaxed and tranquil. When the body becomes relaxed the breath will become calm; when the breath becomes calm the mind will automatically become silent – all these three things are related.

So first we will feel that the body is relaxed – this will make the breathing calm. Then we will feel that the breathing is relaxed – this will make the mind silent.

And then I will give you a third suggestion: that now your mind is becoming silent and empty. In this way, after following each of these three suggestions for a short time, I will say that now the mind has become completely silent. Then for ten minutes you will lie in silence in the same way that you were sitting in silence this morning.

You will hear the cry of a bird, you will hear the sound of a dog and many other sounds – just keep silently listening. It is just as if there is an empty room and a sound comes in, resonates and goes. You should not think about why you are hearing these sounds; neither should you think about why the dog is barking, because you have nothing to do with the dog. There is no reason for you to think about why this dog is barking or why this stupid dog is disturbing you now that you are meditating. No, you have nothing to do with it. The dog does not know at all that you are meditating: he has no idea about it, he is absolutely innocent, he is just doing his job. It is nothing to do with you. He is just barking, so you have to let him bark. It is not a disturbance to you unless you make it a disturbance. It becomes a disturbance only when you resist, when you want the dog to stop barking – the trouble begins there. The dog is barking – it should bark: we are meditating – we should meditate. There is no conflict between these two, there is no opposition. You are silent – the dog's sound will come, linger, and go; it is not a disturbance to you.

Once I was staying in a small village in a rest house. A political leader was also staying with me. That night I don't know what happened, but all the dogs from the village gathered near the rest house and started barking. This politician became very disturbed. He got up, came into my room and asked, "Have you gone to sleep? I am in a great difficulty. I have driven those dogs away twice, but they keep coming back."

I said, "If you drive somebody away they will always come back. It is a mistake to try to drive somebody away, because whoever you drive away thinks that he is needed in some way. He thinks that he has some importance and that is why he is being driven away. And dogs are just poor dogs. They must think that they are needed in some way, that they are important to you, so they came back.

"And the other thing is that the dogs have no idea

that a political leader is staying here, that they are barking for you. They are not human beings – if human beings were to hear that a political leader is here, they would gather around him. Up to now dogs have not become intelligent enough to gather around when a political leader comes. The dogs come here every day. Do not have this foolish idea that is in your mind that they have come here because of your importance. They definitely do not know about it. And as far as the problem of your sleeping is concerned, the dogs are not keeping you awake, you are keeping yourself awake. You are unnecessarily thinking that the dogs should not bark. What right do you have? The dogs have the right to bark and you have the right to sleep. There is no contradiction between them, these things can happen simultaneously. There is no conflict or clash between them. Let the dogs go on barking and you go on sleeping. Neither can the dogs say that you shouldn't sleep because your sleep creates a disturbance to their barking, nor can you say that they disturb you."

And I told him, "Just accept that the dogs are barking and listen silently. Drop the resistance. Accept their barking. And the moment you accept it, the barking of dogs is also transformed into a musical rhythm."

I don't know when he went to sleep, but when he woke up in the morning he said to me, "I don't have any idea what happened, but I am really amazed. When there was nothing else to do I had to accept it. At first your idea made no sense to me" – my ideas do not immediately make sense to anybody, it did not make sense to him either – "but when I felt utterly help-less, I realized there was no other way: I either ruin my sleep or accept what you say. There were only two al-ternatives. Then I thought that as I had given so much attention to the dogs, I should now give attention to your suggestion and see what happens. So I lay down silently and listened, and accepted the barking. After that I have no idea when I fell asleep, and I have no idea how long the dogs kept on barking or when they became silent. I really had a good night's sleep."

So do not resist. Listen silently to whatsoever is all around. This silent listening is a very miraculous phe-nomenon. This non-resistance, this non-opposition towards life is the clue to going into meditation.

So first we will become relaxed and then we will lis-ten silently in a state of non-resistance.The lights will be turned off so that you do not feel that others are present. It is easy to forget the dogs, it is far more diffi-cult to forget the people around you.

CHAPTER FOUR

KNOWING THE MIND

MY BELOVED ONES,

The mind of man has become sick, a wound. It is no longer a healthy center, it has become an unhealthy ulcer. That is why all your attention is concentrated on it. Perhaps you may not have thought about the fact that when a part of the body becomes sick, all one's attention moves towards it.

You only become aware of the leg if there is pain in it; if there is no pain then you are not aware of the leg at all. If there is a wound in the hand then you become aware of the hand; if there is no wound you do not notice it at all. In one way or the other your mind has certainly become sick, because you are aware only of it and nothing else for twenty-four hours a day.

The healthier a body is, the less it will be felt. You feel only that part which has become unhealthy. And the only part of the body which you now feel is the head. Your consciousness only moves around it – only knows it, only recognizes it. A sick wound has appeared there. Without becoming free of this wound, without becoming free of this very tense and very restless state of mind, no person can move towards his center of life. So today we will discuss this state, the mind, and how to change it.

The first thing is that you should clearly understand the state which is mind. If you sit alone for ten minutes and sincerely write down on a piece of paper whatever thoughts are going through your mind, you will be unwilling to show that paper to even your dearest friend – because you will find thoughts which are so mad that neither you nor anyone else could have expected them. You will find such irrelevant, useless and contradictory thoughts that you will think you have gone mad.

If you sincerely write down whatever comes into your mind for ten minutes you will be very surprised at what is happening there. You will wonder if you are sane or crazy. You never look into your mind even for ten minutes to see what is going on there – or maybe it is that you do not look into it because deep down you already know what is happening there. Perhaps you are afraid.

That is why people are afraid of being alone and are looking for company for twenty-four hours a day – wanting to meet friends or go to a club or something. And if they cannot find anybody then they will read a newspaper or listen to the radio. Nobody wants to be alone because the moment you are alone you start finding out about your real state.

When the other is present, you are involved in relating to him and you are not aware of yourself. The search for the other is nothing but the search for an opportunity to escape from yourself. The basic reason that you become interested in other people is that you are afraid of yourself, and you know very well that if you know yourself completely you will find that you are absolutely mad. To escape from this state, man searches for company, searches for companions, searches for a friend, searches for society, searches for a crowd.

Man is afraid of aloneness. He becomes afraid of

aloneness because in aloneness he will find a reflection of his real state, he will come across the reflection of his own face. And it will be very frightening, very scary. So from when he gets up in the morning until he goes to sleep at night, he uses all kinds of methods to escape from himself, so that he does not have to face himself. He is afraid that he may see himself.

Man has invented thousands of ways to escape from himself. And the worse the condition of man's mind has become, the more new inventions he has made to escape from himself. If we look at the last fifty years, we will find that man has created more diversions to escape from himself than ever before in history. The cinemas, the radio, the television, are all ways to escape from oneself. Man has become so restless. Everyone is looking for entertainment; you are doing all kinds of things to forget about yourselves for awhile because your inner situation is becoming worse. All over the world, along with the development of civilization, the use of drugs has increased. Recently new drugs have been discovered which are becoming very popular in Europe and in America. There are drugs like LSD, mescaline, marijuana. In all the cultured cities of Europe and America, among all educated people, the effort to discover new drugs is at its peak. The search to discover reliable means for man to forget himself continues – otherwise man will be in great difficulty.

What is the reason behind all this? Why do you want to forget yourself? Why are you so eager for self-forgetfulness? And don't think that only people who are going to movies are trying to forget themselves: the people who are going to temples are also going for the same reason; there is no difference. The temple is an old way of forgetting oneself, the movie is a new way. If a man is sitting and chanting "Ram, Ram," don't think that he is doing anything other than trying to forget himself in the chanting – just as somebody else is trying to forget himself by listening to a song from a movie. There is no difference between these two people.

The effort to become entangled in anything outside oneself – whether it is "Ram" or a movie or music – the effort to become entangled in anything is deep down nothing but an effort to escape from oneself. You are all engaged in escaping from the self in one way or another. This shows that your condition inside is getting worse, and you are losing the courage even to look at it. You are very afraid to look in that direction.

You are acting like ostriches. Seeing the enemy, an ostrich hides its head in the sand because it thinks it is dangerous to look at the enemy. Because the enemy is not visible the ostrich's logic says, "If it is not visible, it is not there. I am safe." But this logic is wrong. Ostriches can be forgiven, but man cannot be. Simply by not being seen, a thing does not cease to exist. If a thing is visible something can be done about it, but if it is invisible there is no possibility of doing anything.

You want to forget the state which is inside, you don't want to see it. It may be possible to convince your mind that something which is not visible is not there, but that does not mean that it has gone away. There is no relation between not being visible and being non-existent. If something were visible then perhaps you might have been able to change it, but as it is not visible, change is not possible. It will go on growing inside like a wound, like an ulcer which you have hidden and do not want to look at.

The mind has become a wound. If some day a machine is invented with which we can look at what is happening inside each person, everybody will probably commit suicide immediately. Nobody will allow anybody else to see what is going on inside him. Some day or other it will become possible. Right now we can be grateful that there are no windows in our heads through which we can look into each others' minds and see what is going on there.

What people are hiding inside and what they say on the outside are very different. What you see outside on their faces is completely different from what is going on inside them. It is possible that outside they are talking about love, but inside they are full of hate. They may be saying to somebody, "Good morning. I am pleased to see you. I am happy that I met you this morning" – but inside they are saying, "Why do I have to see the face of this stupid person first thing in the morning?"

If there were windows to look into people's heads we would be in a great difficulty, life would become really difficult to live. We might be talking to someone in a friendly manner but thinking inside, "When is this man going to die?" There is one thing on the surface and something else underneath – and we don't dare to look inward, to look inside and see.

A mother and her daughter lived together and both of them walked in their sleep. One night at about three o'clock the mother got up and went into the garden behind the house. After awhile her daughter also got up in her sleep and walked into the garden. As soon as the old woman saw her daughter she shouted, "Bitch! You have taken away my youth. From the time you were born, I started growing old. You are my enemy. If you had not been born I would still be young."

And when the girl saw her mother she shouted, "You wicked woman. Because of you my life has become difficult, a bondage. You have always been a rock in the flow of my life. You are a heavy chain around my neck."

At that moment the cock crowed and they both woke up. Seeing the girl the old women said, "Dear. Why did you get up so early? You might catch cold. Come, let's go inside."

Immediately the girl touched the feet of her old mother. She had a habit of touching the feet of her mother every morning. She said, "Mother! You got up so early. Your health is not good. You should not get up so early. Come and rest."

You can see the difference between what they said in their sleep and when they were awake.

Whatever a man says in his sleep is more authentic

than what he says when he is awake, because it is more from the inside. What you see of yourself in your dreams is more of a reality than what you see in the marketplace and in the crowd. The face in the crowd is made up and artificial; deep down within yourself you are a totally different person. You may manage to hide things by sticking some good thoughts on the surface, but inside the fire of thoughts is burning. On the surface you may seem absolutely silent and healthy, but inside everything is unhealthy and disturbed. On the surface you seem to be smiling, but it is possible that the smile is just covering an ocean of tears. In fact, it is likely that you have been practicing your smiles just to hide the tears within. This is usually what people do.

Somebody once asked Nietzsche, "You are always laughing. You are so joyous. Do you really feel this way?"

Nietzsche said, "Now that you have asked, I will tell you the reality. I am laughing so that I don't start crying instead. Before my crying can start, I suppress it by laughing. I stop it inside myself. My laughter must convince others that I am happy. And I laugh only because I am so sad that I feel a relief by laughing. Sometimes I can console myself."

Nobody has seen Buddha laughing, nobody has seen Mahavira laughing, nobody has seen Christ laughing. There must be a reason. Perhaps there are no tears inside so there is no need to laugh to hide them. Perhaps inside no sorrow remains to be hidden by smiling. Whatever was disturbed inside has disappeared, so now there is no need to stick the flowers of laughter on the outside.

Someone whose body stinks needs to sprinkle perfume on it. Someone whose body is ugly needs to make an effort to look beautiful. Someone who is sad within has to learn to laugh, and someone who is filled with tears inside has to keep smiling on the outside. Someone who is full of thorns within must stick flowers on himself outside.

Man is absolutely not as he appears to be, he is the total opposite. He is one thing on the inside and something else on the outside. And it is alright if others are deceived by what you have stuck on the outside, but the problem is that you yourself are deceived by it. If only others were deceived by the outer appearance it would be alright – it is not very surprising because people usually only see the outside. But you yourself are deceived because you think you really are the image that other people see. You look at yourself through the eyes of the other, you never see yourself directly as you are, as you authentically are.

The image formed in other people's eyes deceives you and you become afraid to look within. You want to see the image people have of you, not your reality. What are people saying? – you become very interested in knowing what people say about you. There is nothing else behind this curiosity to know: you think you can recognize yourself through the image formed in others' eyes. This is really surprising! Even to know yourself you have to look into another person's eyes.

People are afraid that others might say something bad about them. They feel happy if people say something good about them because their knowledge of themselves depends on others' opinion. They do not have immediate knowledge of themselves; they do not have any direct experience of knowing themselves. This experience could happen, but it doesn't because you try to escape from it.

The first thing in encountering the mind is not to bother about what others say or how you appear to others; rather, you have to have a direct encounter with what you essentially are. In your aloneness you have to open your mind totally and see what is there. It is an act of courage. It is an act of tremendous courage to decide to enter into the hell hidden within yourself. It is an act of great courage to see yourself in your nudity. Great courage is needed.

Once there was an emperor. Every day he used to disappear into a room in the middle of his palace. His family, the people in his house, his friends, his ministers were all surprised about this habit. He used to always keep the key of that room with him, and when he went into the room he would lock the door from the inside. There was only one door to the room and not a single window. During a period of twenty-four hours he would stay in that room for at least one hour.

Even his wives did not know anything about the room because he had never told anybody about it. If somebody asked he would smile and remain silent, and he would not give the key to anybody. All the people were surprised about it and their curiosity went on growing every day: "What does he do there?" Nobody knew. He used to stay in that closed room for one hour, then he would come out silently and put the key in his pocket, and the next day he would do the same thing again. At last the people's curiosity reached a peak and they conspired with each other to find out what he was doing. His ministers, his wives, his sons, his daughters were part of the conspiracy.

One night they made a hole in the wall so that they would be able to see what he was doing when he next went there. The next day, when the emperor went inside, they all peeped through the hole one by one. But whoever put his eye to the hole immediately moved aside and said, "What is he doing? What is he doing?" But nobody could say what he was doing.

The emperor had gone inside and taken off all his clothes. Then he spread his hands towards the sky and said, "Oh, God! The person who was wearing these clothes is not me. That is not my reality – *this* is my reality." And he started jumping and shouting and screaming abuses and behaving like a madman.

Whoever looked through the hole moved aside immediately, in shock, and said, "What is our emperor doing? We used to think that perhaps he would be doing some yoga or saying some prayers. But this! What is he doing?"

And the emperor said to God, "The silent and peaceful-looking person who was standing clothed in front of you is absolutely false. He was a cultivated man. I made him that way through my efforts. In reality, I am like this. This is my reality, this is my nakedness and this is my madness. If you accept my reality then it is alright – because I can deceive people, but how can I deceive you? I can show people that I am not naked by wearing clothes, but you know very well that I am naked. How can I deceive you? I can show people that I am very silent and blissful, but you know me in my very depth. How can I deceive you? In front of you I am just a madman."

In front of God we are all like madmen. In fact, leave God aside – if we look within ourselves then even to our own eyes we will look like madmen. Our minds have become absolutely confused, but we have never paid any attention to this problem so we have not developed any methods to deal with it.

The first thing is to encounter the mind directly. But for this encounter to happen, you must understand two or three points. After that you will be able to think about how the mind can be changed.

The first thing for a direct encounter with the mind is that you should drop all your fears about knowing yourself. What is the fear of knowing yourself? The fear is that perhaps you are a bad person. The fear is that you may discover that you are a bad person after having cultivated an image of being a good person. You appear to be a good person – you are saintly, you are innocent, you are authentic, you are truthful. Your fear is that you may realize that inside you are not authentic, false. You are afraid of finding out that you are irreligious, complicated, cunning, hypocritical, unsaintly. The fear is that the image of yourself – what you think yourself to be – may turn out to be false.

A person who is afraid in this way can never encounter the mind. It is very easy to go into the forests, it is easy to go into darkness, it is easy to sit fearlessly in front of wild animals, but it is very difficult to stand fearlessly in front of the wild man that is hidden within you. It is very arduous. It is not at all difficult to stand for years in the sun – any fool can do that; it is not difficult to stand on your head – any idiot can be taught such circus tricks; and it is not very difficult to lie down on thorns – the skin adjusts to the thorns very soon. If there is one thing that is really arduous, it is to find the courage to have an immediate experience of what you are within – whether bad or mad, however you are.

So the first thing is to drop fear and to get ready to see yourself courageously. One who does not have this courage is in trouble. You are interested in attaining to the soul, you are interested in knowing existence, but you do not have the courage to have a direct and simple encounter with yourself. The soul and existence are very far away: the first reality is your mind. The first reality is the thought center with which you are most closely related: one has first to see it, know it, recognize it.

The first thing is the effort to know your own mind in aloneness, without fear. For at least half an hour every day give your mind a chance to express itself as it is. Close yourself in a room – like the emperor – and give total freedom to your mind. Tell it, "Whatsoever you want to think, to contemplate, let it happen." Drop all the censoring of yourself that has prevented things from surfacing – drop all that. Give your mind the freedom to allow whatever arises to arise, to allow whatever appears to appear. Don't stop or suppress anything – you are ready to know what is inside.

And you should also not judge what is good or bad because the moment you judge, suppression begins. Whatever you call bad, the mind starts suppressing, and whatever you call good, the mind starts using as a cover-up. So you don't need to judge anything as either good or bad. Whatever is there in the mind, however it is, be prepared to know it as it is.

If you let your mind be totally free to think, to contemplate, to feel, you will feel very frightened and wonder if you are mad. But it is essential to know what is hidden inside in order to be free from it. Knowledge and recognition are the first steps to getting free from it. You cannot conquer an enemy which you do not know or recognize; there is no way. The hidden enemy, the enemy standing behind you, is more dangerous than the enemy in front of you that you are acquainted with, that you recognize.

The first thing is that because of the restrictions and inhibitions that you have imposed on the mind from all sides, you don't let the mind express itself in its spontaneity. You have restricted all its spontaneity.

Everything has become unnatural and false. You have covered everything in veils, you are wearing false faces and you never allow the mind to express itself directly.

So in the beginning at least allow the mind to express itself directly, in front of you, so that you become acquainted with all the contents which have been hidden and suppressed. A great part of the mind has been suppressed in darkness. You never take a lamp there. You live on the balcony of your own house and inside there is darkness in all the rooms, and you don't know how many insects and spiders and snakes and scorpions are hidden there. In darkness, they are bound to gather. And you are afraid to take a light there; you don't even want to think about the condition of your house.

It is absolutely essential for a seeker to drop this fear. To bring about a revolution in your mind and thoughts, the first thing is to drop the fear, to be ready to know yourself without fear. The second thing is to get rid of all the censorship and restrictions you have imposed on the mind – and you have imposed many restrictions on it. Your education, your moral preachings, your civilization and culture have imposed many restrictions – "Don't think about this. Don't allow a thought of this kind to enter your mind. It is a bad thought! Don't allow it!" When you suppress them, bad thoughts are not destroyed – they only go deeper into your subconscious.

By suppression, a thought does not leave, it goes more deeply into your being – because what you are suppressing came from within, it did not come from somewhere outside.

Remember, whatever is there in your mind does not come from somewhere outside, it comes from within. It is as if a spring is coming out of a mountain and we close its opening: the spring will not be destroyed; it will go deeper and it will search for other ways to come out of the mountain. Originally there would have been one spring, but now perhaps there will be ten because the water will try to flow out by splitting into ten springs. And if you close these ten places then there will be a hundred springs.

Everything comes from within, not from the outside. And the more you suppress it the more ugly and perverted it becomes. Then it finds new ways to come out, new complications are created – but you go on suppressing it more strongly. From your very childhood the basis of your education is that if a certain thought in the mind is wrong, suppress it. That suppressed thought is not destroyed, it enters deeper into your subconscious. And the more you go on suppressing it the deeper it goes and the more power it has over you.

Anger is wrong so you suppress it: then a current of anger spreads right through you. Sex is wrong, greed is wrong, this is wrong, that is wrong.... Whatsoever is wrong you suppress, and in the end you find that you have become whatsoever you had suppressed. How long can you block those suppressed springs by closing their openings?

And the mind functions in certain ways. For example, whatever you want to suppress or escape from becomes central to the mind. Whatever you want to escape from becomes an attraction, and the mind starts moving towards it. Try it! – if you try to escape from something or suppress something, the mind will immediately become focused on it.

Milarepa was a mystic who lived in Tibet. One day a young man went to him and said, "I want to attain some powers. Please give me a mantra."

Milarepa said, "We don't have any mantras. We are mystics. Mantras are for magicians, for jugglers – go to them. We don't have any mantras – why should we need powers?"

But the more Milarepa refused the more the young man thought that there must be something there – "Why else should he refuse?" So he kept returning to Milarepa again and again.

Great crowds always gather around saints who drive people away with sticks or throw stones at them. The crowds think that the saint must have something special, otherwise he would not be driving people away. But you don't realize that attracting people through an advertisement in a newspaper or through throwing stones at them is the same trick; the propaganda is the same. And the second way is more manipulative and cunning. When people are driven away by someone throwing stones they don't understand that they are actually being attracted: this is a subtle way of doing it. And the people do come although they have no idea that they have been seduced.

The young man thought that perhaps Milarepa was

trying to hide something, so he started coming every day. In the end Milarepa got fed up so he wrote a mantra on a piece of paper for him and said, "Take this. Tonight is the night of no moon. Read this five times during the night. If you read it five times, you will get the power you want. Then you will be able to do whatever you want to do. Now go and leave me alone."

The young man grabbed the paper, turned around and ran. He did not even thank Milarepa. But he had not descended the steps of the temple when Milarepa called after him, "My friend. I forgot to tell you one thing. There is a certain condition attached to this mantra. When you read it, you should not have any thoughts in your mind about a monkey."

The young man said, "Don't be worried, I have never had such a thought in my whole life. There has never been any reason to think of a monkey. I have to read this only five times, there is no problem."

But he was mistaken – he had not even descended to the bottom of the steps when the monkeys started coming. He became very scared. He closed his eyes and there were monkeys inside; he looked outside and he saw monkeys even where there were no monkeys. It was already night and every movement in the trees seemed to be a monkey. It seemed that monkeys were everywhere. By the time he got home he was very worried because up until then he had never thought about monkeys; he had never had anything to do with them.

He took a bath, but while he was bathing the monkeys were with him. His whole mind was obsessed with only one thing – monkeys. Then he sat down to read the mantra. He picked up the paper, closed his eyes – and there was a crowd of monkeys inside teasing him. He became very much afraid, but still he persevered the whole night. He changed his positions; he tried to sit in this way, in that way, in *padmasana*, in *siddhasana*, in other different yoga postures. He prayed, he bowed, he begged. He cried out to anybody to help him get rid of these monkeys, but the monkeys were adamant; they were not ready to leave him that night.

By the morning the young man was almost mad with fear, and he realized that the mantra power could not be attained so easily. He saw that Milarepa had been very clever, he had put a difficult condition on him. Milarepa was crazy! If there was going to be a hindrance because of the monkeys, then at least he should not have mentioned them. Then perhaps the mantra power could have been attained.

In the morning he went back to Milarepa crying and said, "Take your mantra back. You have made a big mistake. If monkeys were a hindrance in using this mantra, then you should not have mentioned them. I never usually think of monkeys, but the whole of last night the monkeys chased me. Now I will have to wait for my next life to attain this mantra power because in this life this mantra and the monkeys have become one. Now it is not possible to get rid of them."

The monkeys had become one with the mantra. How did this happen? – his mind insisted that the monkeys should not be there, and so the monkeys came. Whenever his mind tried to get rid of the monkeys, the monkeys appeared. Whenever his mind tried to escape from the monkeys the monkeys came.

To forbid is to attract, to refuse is to invite, to prevent is to tempt.

Your mind has become very sick because you don't understand this simple point. You don't want to be angry – then anger comes like a monkey. You don't want to be sexual – then sex appears like a monkey and gets a grip on your being. You don't want greed, you don't want ego – and they all come. But what-ever you want – spirituality, religiousness, enlightenment – does not seem to come. That which you don't want comes, and that which you try to get never appears. All this frustration happens because of not understanding this simple point about the mind.

The second thing to remember is that there is no need to insist on what should be in the mind and what should not. We should be ready to watch whatsoever appears in our minds without making any choices and without any conditions. In this way we can begin to see what the mind is, in reality.

The simple fact of the contradictory nature of the mind is well understood by advertisers around the world, but religious leaders have not understood it at all. Propagandists all over the world understand this fact, but the people teaching in society have not understood it. When a movie is advertised 'for adults only', children go to it with a few pennies worth of false mustache

stuck on their faces. The advertisers know that to attract children it is necessary to use the words 'for adults
only' on the advertisement. There are women's magazines 'for women only'. Nobody reads them except
men; women never read them. I enquired about it and
found out that most of the buyers are men. And when I
asked the agents about the magazines they sell in the
market they said, "Women buy magazines marked 'for
women only' just once in a while; they usually buy
magazines that are labeled 'for men only'."

The advertisers understand what attracts man's
mind, but the religious leaders and the teachers of
morality have not understood it yet. They still go on
teaching people stupidities like, "Don't be angry, fight
with the anger." A person fighting with his anger and
trying to escape from it will be obsessed with anger his
whole life. He can never be free from it. Only a person
who is interested in knowing his anger face-to-face and
not fighting it will become free of it.

So the second point to remember is to drop all the
feelings of conflict and struggle with any state of mind.
Just create a feeling of wanting to know, to understand
– "I should understand what my mind is." One should
enter the mind with this kind of sincere feeling. That is
the second point.

And the third point is not to make any judgment
about whatsoever arises in the mind. Don't make any
judgement about what is bad or what is good. Badness
and goodness are two sides of the same coin. Wherever there is badness, there is goodness on the other

side; wherever there is goodness, there is badness on the other side.

A bad person is hidden inside a good person and a good person is hidden inside a bad person. A good person has the good side of his coin facing upwards and the bad side facing downwards. So if a good person becomes bad, then he proves to be worse than the most bad person. And if a bad person becomes good, then a good person seems pale in comparison. In a bad person, the goodness has been completely hidden – only the badness shows. If he changes and becomes a good man, then other good people will look pale next to him. A very fresh and hidden force of goodness arises from within him. Valmiki or Angulimal are good examples: they were very bad people who one day became good, and they outshone all other saints with their goodness.

A good person and a bad person are not different; they are two sides of the same coin. But a sage is a third kind of person – inside him there is neither goodness nor badness. The coin disappears altogether. A sage is not a good man or a gentleman or a saint. A wicked man is always hidden inside a gentleman, and a gentleman is always hidden inside a bad man. A sage is absolutely a third type of phenomenon. He is beyond both good and bad; he has no relation to either one. He has entered a totally different dimension where there is no question of good and bad.

A young monk lived in a village in Japan. He was

very famous and had a great reputation. The whole village worshiped and respected him. Songs were sung all over the village in his honor. But one day everything changed. A young girl in the village became pregnant and gave birth to a child. When her family asked her whose child it was, she said it was the child of the young monk.

How long does it take for admirers to become enemies? How long? It does not take even a moment because inside the mind of an admirer, condemnation is always hidden. The mind just waits for a chance, and the day admiration ends condemnation begins. Those people who show respect can change to being disrespectful in one minute. The people who are touching someone's feet can start cutting the same person's head off within a moment. There is no difference between respect and disrespect – they are two faces of the same coin.

The people of the whole village attacked the monk's hut. For a long time they had been showing respect to him but now all the anger that they had suppressed came out. Now they had the chance to be disrespectful, so they all ran to the monk's hut and set it on fire, and threw the tiny baby at him.

The monk asked, "What is the matter?"

The people shouted, "You are asking us what is the matter? This child is yours. Do we have to tell you what is the matter? Look at your burning house, look within your heart, look at this child and look at this girl. There is no need for us to tell you that this child is yours."

The monk said, "Is it so? Is this child mine?"

The child started crying so he started singing a song to make the child silent, and the people left him sitting by his burned-out hut. Then he went to beg at his usual time, in the afternoon – but who would give him food today? Today every door he stood in front of was slammed shut. Today a crowd of children and people started walking behind him teasing him, throwing stones. He reached the house of the girl whose child it was. He said, "I may not get food for myself, but at least give some milk for this child! I may be at fault, but what is the fault of this poor baby?"

The child was crying, the crowd was standing there – and it became unbearable for the girl. She fell at the feet of her father and said, "Forgive me, I lied when I gave the name of the monk. I wanted to save the real father of the child so I thought of using the name of this monk. I don't even have any acquaintance with him."

The father became nervous – this was a great mistake. He ran out of his house, fell at the feet of the monk and tried to take the baby from him.

The monk asked, "What is the matter?"

The girl's father said, "Forgive me, there has been a mistake. The child is not yours."

The monk replied, "Is this so? Is the child really not mine?"

Then the people of the village said to him, "You are mad! Why didn't you deny it this morning?"

The monk said, "What difference would it have

made? The child must belong to somebody. And you had already burned one hut – you would have just burned one more. You had enjoyed abusing one person, you would have enjoyed abusing one more. What difference would it make? The child must belong to someone – it could also be mine. So what is the problem? What difference does it make?"

The people said, "Don't you understand that everybody condemned you, insulted you, totally humiliated you?"

The monk answered, "If I had been concerned about your condemnation, I would have been concerned about your respect also. I do as I feel right, you do whatever you feel to be right. Until yesterday you felt it right to respect me, so you did. Today you felt it right not to respect me, so you didn't. But I am not concerned with either your respect or your disrespect."

The people said to him, "Oh, honorable monk, you should at least have considered that you would lose your good reputation."

He replied, "I am neither bad nor good. I am simply myself. I have dropped this idea of good and bad. I have dropped all concern about becoming good because the more I tried to become good, the more I found that I became bad. The more I tried to escape from badness the more I found that goodness was disappearing, so I dropped the very idea. I became absolutely indifferent. And the day I became indifferent I found that neither goodness nor badness remained inside. Rather, something new was born which is better than goodness and which does not even have a shadow of badness about it."

A sage is a third type of person. The journey of a seeker is not one of becoming a good man; the journey of a seeker is one of becoming a sage.

So my third point is: do not decide that a thought which is arising in the mind is good or bad. Don't condemn or appreciate. Don't say that this is bad or this is good. Just sit on the side of the stream of the mind, as if you are sitting on the bank of a river and indifferently watching the flow. Water is flowing, stones are flowing, leaves are flowing, wood is flowing, and you are watching, sitting silently on the bank.

These are the three points I wanted to tell you about this morning. The first thing is tremendous fearlessness in encountering the mind; the second thing is no restrictions, no conditions on the mind; the third point is no judgments about whatsoever thoughts and longings arise in the mind, no judgements of good or bad. Your attitude should simply be indifferent. These three points are necessary in order to understand the perversions of the mind. Then in the afternoon and evening we will talk about what can be done to get rid of these perversions and go beyond – but these three basic points have to be kept in mind.

Now we will get ready for the morning meditation.

First, there are two points to understand about the morning meditation, then we will sit for it. The morning meditation is a very direct and simple process. Actually, whatever is significant in life is very simple and direct. In life, the more meaningless a thing is, the more complicated and complex it is. In life, the higher a thing is the more simple and direct it is.

It is a very direct and simple process. The only thing you have to do is to sit silently and listen silently to the world of sound all around. Listening has some wonderful effects. Usually we never listen. When I am speaking here, if you think that you are listening then you are making a great mistake. A sound falling on the ear is not the meaning of listening.

If when I am talking, at the same time you are thinking, then you are not listening because the mind can do only one thing at a time, never two things. Either you can listen or you can think. As long as you are thinking, for that much time listening will stop; as long as you are listening, for that much time thinking will stop. So when I say that listening is a wonderful process, what I mean is if you just listen silently then the thinking will stop on its own – because it is one of the essential rules of the mind that it is incapable of doing two things at a time, absolutely incapable.

A man had fallen sick. For one year his legs had been paralyzed. The doctors told him that there was no paralysis in his body, it was his mind imagining it. But how could he agree? – he was paralyzed. Then his house caught fire. As it burned, all the people in the house ran out – and the paralyzed man also ran. He had not been out of his bed for one year. As he ran he thought, "My

God! How did this happen? For one year I was not even able to get up. How can I be walking now?"

The man asked me about it and I told him, "Mind cannot think of two things at the same time. The paralysis was a thought of the mind, but when the house caught on fire the mind became totally involved with the fire so the first thought – that my legs are paralyzed – disappeared and you ran out of the house! The mind can be intensely aware about only one thing at a time."

This morning's experiment is about listening silently to the songs of the birds and the wind, to the whole cacophony of all the sounds around you. Listen to them very silently. Give attention to only one thing: "I am listening. I am listening totally to whatever is happening. I am not doing anything else, just listening, totally listening."

I am stressing listening because as you listen totally, the continuous movement of thoughts within you will become absolutely silent – because both of these things cannot happen simultaneously. So put your total effort into listening. This is a positive effort.

If you try to throw out the thoughts then the mistake which I just told you about will start happening. It is a negative effort. Thoughts cannot be thrown out by making an effort to get rid of them, but if the energy of the mind which usually goes into thinking starts flowing into some other stream, then thoughts will automatically become weak.

The doctors of the paralyzed man used to tell him, "Drop the idea from your mind that you are paralyzed.

You are not really paralyzed. But the more the man tried to throw out the thought that he was paralyzed, the more he would be reminded of his paralysis. "If I am not paralyzed then why am I repeating, 'I am not paralyzed'?" Every time he repeated, "I am not paralyzed," he was deepening and strengthening his feeling that he was paralyzed. The mind of this man needed a diversion. There was no need for him to try to stop his thought about paralysis. If he had had the opportunity to get involved in something else, then his paralysis would have disappeared because it was a paralysis of the mind, not of the body. It was necessary for his mind to totally move aside for the paralysis to disappear.

Fortunately, his house caught on fire. It may happen that what looks like a disaster later on proves to be a lucky happening. This time it was lucky that the man's house caught fire because his whole attention went suddenly to the fire. His mind shifted from the paralysis which it was holding on to, and the illusion suddenly disappeared. It was an illusion, no more than that. In reality, there were no chains, there was only a web of thoughts. When the man's mind became distracted his thoughts dried up and became lifeless – because thoughts get their life from your attention.

Thoughts have no life of their own. The more attention you give to a thought, the more alive it becomes. The more you remove your attention, the more dead it becomes. If attention is totally withdrawn then thoughts become lifeless: they die, they disappear immediately.

That is why I am saying that you should give all your

attention to listening. Decide absolutely that even the smallest voice of a bird should not go unheard, should not be missed. You should hear everything, whatever is happening all around – you should hear it all. Then you will suddenly find that the mind is entering into a deep silence, the thoughts are fading away.

Only one thing has to be done: you have simply to relax your body. Yesterday I told you to first tense your mind, but perhaps you misunderstood. Relax your mind, do not tense it. That is not necessary – because if you get caught up in the idea of tensing the mind, then that itself will become a problem. So drop that idea; it was not a part of the meditation. I had told you to do that just so that you could get some idea of what a tense mind and what a relaxed mind are. There is no need to worry about this idea. Drop it. And now relax. Let the mind be relaxed. Relax all the tense tissues and nerves of your brain. It is a matter of relaxing. The question is not of learning the art of making the mind tense. You need to forget the art of keeping the mind tense. I told you that just so that you can understand the contrast between your mind being tense and being relaxed. For now, drop whatever you cannot understand. Just simply relax it.

So everybody please sit, keeping some distance from each other. Nobody should be touching anyone. Use this space in front. Come up here or go to the back, but nobody should be touching anyone else.

Allow the body to be totally relaxed and then slowly close the eyes. The eyes have to be closed so gently that there is no strain on the eyes. You should not close the eyes tightly, otherwise you will feel a strain. The muscles of the eyes are very much related to the mind, so let them be absolutely relaxed. Let your eyelids fall in the same way small children's do. Let the eyelids fall slowly, relaxedly. Then relax all the muscles of the face and head. You have seen the face of a small child, absolutely relaxed, nothing tense. Make your face like that – absolutely loose and relaxed. Let the body also be relaxed. The moment you let everything relax the breath will become relaxed and silent on its own.

Then do only one thing: listen silently to whatever sounds are coming from all around. A crow will make a sound, a bird will make a sound, a child will speak on the road – listen to them silently. Go on listening and listening and listening, and everything will become silent inside.

Listen – listen silently for ten minutes. Let all the attention be on listening.

Be just listening, doing nothing else.

Listen...the birds are singing, the winds are shaking the trees – whatever sounds may come, listen to them silently.

Listen...and by and by, within you, a humming of silence will begin.

The mind is becoming silent. Go on listening and listening. The mind is becoming silent, the mind is becoming silent...the mind is becoming silent....

The mind has become silent, the mind has become absolutely silent. A deep silence is present inside. Listen to it, just listen to it. Listen...and by and by the mind will become silent.

The mind is becoming silent, the mind is becoming silent, the mind is becoming silent. Go on listening and listening, the mind is entering an absolute silence....

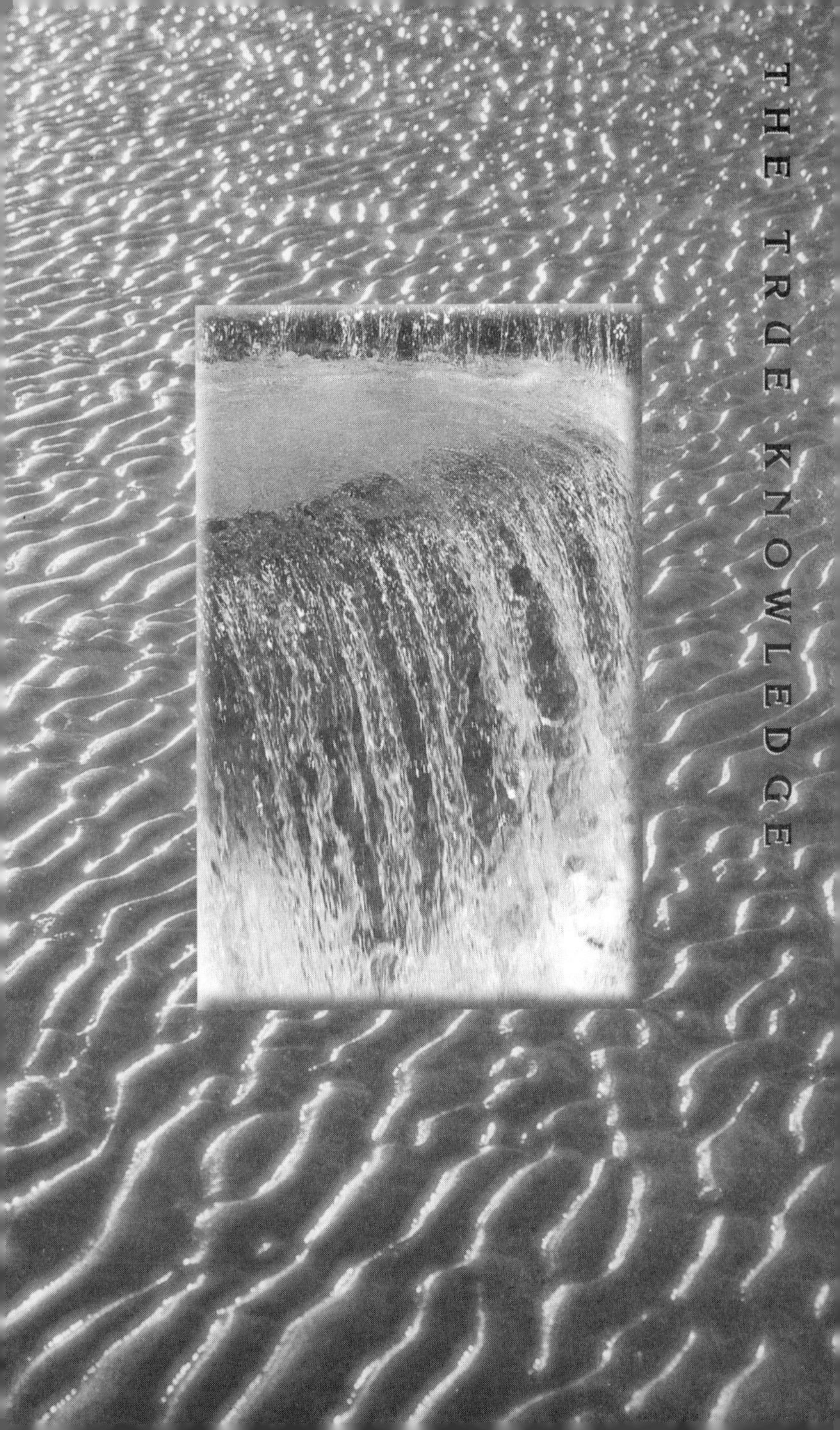
THE TRUE KNOWLEDGE

CHAPTER FIVE

THE TRUE KNOWLEDGE

My BELOVED ONES,

The state of man's mind is like a disturbed hive of honeybees: thoughts and thoughts and thoughts buzz round and round. Surrounded by these thoughts, man lives in anxiety, tension and worry. To recognize and to know life, mind needs to be silent like a lake in which there are no ripples. To be acquainted with life, mind needs to be clear like a mirror on which there is no dust.

You have a mind like a hive of honeybees: it is neither a mirror nor a silent lake. If you think that you will be able to know something with such a mind, that you will be able to attain to something or that you will be able to become something, you are making a great mistake. It is absolutely necessary to become free from this constant flow of thoughts.

To have thoughts and thoughts and thoughts buzzing around is not a sign of health, it is the sign of a sick mind. When one's mind is totally pure and clean, when it is healthy, then thoughts disappear. Consciousness remains but thoughts disappear. When mind is sick and unhealthy, then consciousness disappears and only a crowd of thoughts remains. You live in that crowd of thoughts. From morning until evening, from evening until morning, from birth until death, you live in a crowd of thoughts.

How can you get free of this crowd of thoughts? I said a few things about this in the morning, and some questions have been asked in connection with what I said. I will now answer those questions.

The first thing is that becoming free of thoughts is the second step: the first step is not to create a crowd of thoughts in the first place. If you go on collecting thoughts on the one hand and try to become free of thoughts on the other hand, how will you manage? If you want to get rid of the leaves of a tree and you go on giving water to the roots of the tree, then how will you be able to get rid of the leaves of the tree? Watering the roots, you don't seem to realize that there is a relationship between the roots and the leaves – a deep relationship. The roots and leaves seem to be separate, but the leaves are not separate from the roots and the water which is given to the roots reaches all the way up to the leaves.

So you collect many thoughts and water their roots, and then when these thoughts leave the mind feeling very uneasy and disturbed, you want to' find a way to silence them. But to stop the tree from growing leaves you have to stop giving water to its roots. You should understand how you water the roots of your thoughts. If you come to understand this, you can stop it. Then it will not be long before the leaves wither away.

How do you water your thoughts?

For thousands of years man has had the illusion that he can attain to knowledge by accumulating other people's thoughts. This is absolutely false and wrong – no one can ever attain to knowledge by accumulating other people's thoughts. Knowledge comes from the inside and thoughts come from the outside. Knowledge is yours and thoughts are always from others, always borrowed. Knowledge is the throbbing of your own being, it is the surfacing of that which is hidden within yourself. Thoughts are a collection of what others have said – you can collect them from the Gita, from the Koran, from the Bible or from any teachers and religious leaders.

Whatever you get from other people does not become your knowledge, it becomes ways and means with which you hide your ignorance. And when a man's ignorance is hidden he can never attain to knowledge. Because you have the idea that this is your knowledge, you cling to it with your whole being. You cling to your thoughts, you are not courageous enough to drop them. You support them because you think they are your knowledge and that if you lose them you will become ignorant. But remember that howsoever much you may cling to your thoughts, you do not become a knower through these thoughts.

When someone digs a well, he first takes out the soil and stones and then water seeps in from the sides of the well and fills it. The water was already there, it did not need to be brought from anywhere else. Only some stones and layers of soil needed to be removed. There were some hindrances, some obstacles: once they were removed the water appeared. It was not necessary to bring water to the well, it was already there – just some hindrances had to be removed.

Knowledge is already present inside, it does not have

to be obtained from somewhere else. Its springs are hidden inside; only the obstacles in between – the stones and the soil – have to be removed by digging. Then the springs of knowledge will start appearing.

But one can make a well and one can make a pond. Making a pond is different. You do not need to look for a natural source of water to make a pond. The way to make a pond is completely opposite to that of making a well. To make a pond you do not need to dig out stones and soil, you have to bring them from somewhere else and make a wall of them. And when the wall has been built the water does not come by itself: you have to take water from other people's wells and put it in the pond. On the surface, a pond gives the illusion of a well. It appears to be a well. You can see water in a pond and you can also see water in a well, but the difference between a pond and a well is the same as the difference between the earth and sky. The first difference is that a pond has no water of its own.

No thirst in this world is quenched by something that is not one's own. Whatever is in a pond is borrowed: it soon becomes stale and stagnant because that which is borrowed is not alive, it is dead. The water standing in the pond becomes stagnant, rotten, and will soon start stinking.

But a well has its own source of water, the water never becomes stagnant. A well has its own flowing source.

Two different processes are happening with a pond and a well. A pond is afraid that somebody will take its water away because if its water goes, it will become empty. And a well wants someone to take its water so that more fresh water can fill it, fresh and more alive. A well calls out, "Take my water, I want to share it," and a pond calls out, "Keep away. Don't touch my water, don't take my water!" A pond wants somebody who has water to bring it and pour it in so its wealth can grow. But if somebody has a bucket, the well wants that person to take some of its water so that it can get rid of the water which has become old and get new water. A well wants to share, a pond wants to hoard. A well has streams which are connected to the ocean. A well seems to be small, but deep inside it is connected with the infinite. And howsoever big a pond may look, it has no relation to anyone – it ends in itself and is closed. It has no stream; it has no way of connecting with the infinite.

If somebody goes to the pond and talks about the ocean, the pond will laugh and say, "There is no such thing as an ocean. Everything is a pond. There is no ocean anywhere." A pond has no idea about the ocean.

But if somebody praises the beauty of the well the well will think, "What is mine? Everything comes from the ocean. What am I? Whatever comes to me is connected far away with something else." A well cannot have any 'I' of its own, any feeling of 'I am', but a pond has an ego and a feeling of 'I am'. And the interesting thing is that a well is very big but a pond is very small; a well has its own wealth but a pond has no wealth of its own.

Man's mind can become a well or a pond: these are the only two possibilities of how man's mind can evolve. And a person whose mind becomes a pond, slowly, slowly will become mad.

All of your minds have become ponds. You have not created wells, you have created ponds. You collect things from all over the world – from books, from scriptures, from teachings – you collect all of them and think that you have become learned. You have made the same mistake as the pond. The pond thought that it was a well, and the illusion can be created because you can see that there is water in both of them.

You can find knowledge in a scholar, a teacher and in a conscious person, but a scholar is a pond and a conscious person is a well. There is a great difference between the two. You cannot imagine how fundamental and how deep this difference is. The knowledge of a scholar is borrowed, stale, rotten. The troubles that have arisen in the world are because of the scholars' knowledge. Whose fight is the fight between Hindus and Mohammedans – it is the fight of scholars. The opposition between a Jaina and a Hindu is the opposition between scholars. It is an opposition of scholars – it is an opposition of minds which are rotten, borrowed and stale.

All the troubles that have happened all over the world are because of minds which have become ponds. Otherwise there are just people in the world – nobody is a Christian, a Hindu, a Mohammedan, a Jaina. These are just labels for the ponds. The pond puts a label on itself, a label of the well from which it has drawn its water – someone has drawn water from the Gita so he is a Hindu; someone has drawn water from the Koran so he is a Mohammedan.

A conscious person does not take water from others, the water comes from within him. It comes from existence, so he can be neither a Hindu, a Mohammedan nor a Christian. A conscious person cannot belong to any sect, but a scholar cannot be without a sect. Whenever you find a scholar he will belong to a sect.

You have made your mind a stale, borrowed thing – and then you cling to it. As I said, a pond shouts, "Do not take away my water! If the water is gone then I will become empty, there will be nothing left inside me. My wealth is borrowed so nobody should take it away."

Remember, the wealth which decreases when it is used is always borrowed and false, and the wealth which increases when it is used is true. Wealth which is depleted by sharing is not wealth at all; it is only an accumulation. Only wealth which increases by sharing is really wealth. Hence, the nature of wealth is such that it will increase when it is shared. If it decreases when it is shared, then it is not wealth. And then too, someone who is afraid that his wealth will disappear through sharing must take great care of his wealth. So all borrowed wealth is a problem. Because it is never real, fear arises that it will disappear and so you cling to it more tightly.

You cling tightly to your thoughts. You care for them more than for your life. All this garbage which has accumulated in your mind did not get there just by chance: you have arranged it, you have collected it and you are taking care of it.

So if you think that knowledge arises with the accumulation of thoughts you will never be able to become free from them. How can you become free? It would be like giving water to the roots and then cutting the leaves – it cannot happen.

So the first basic thing that has to be understood is that knowledge and your collection of thoughts are two different things. Thoughts acquired or borrowed from others is not knowledge. Thoughts taken from other sources do not lead a man to truth or to himself. This knowledge is false, it is pseudo-knowledge. It creates an illusion that you have attained to knowledge, but in reality nothing is known, you remain ignorant.

This situation is the same as somebody reading many books about swimming, and learning so much about it that if he had to give a discourse on swimming or write a book about it, he could – but if somebody pushes him into a river it will become obvious that he cannot swim. He has read and learned all about it, he knows all the theory, but in practice he cannot swim.

There was a Mohammedan *fakir* called Nasruddin. Once, when he was sitting in a boat crossing a river, he and the boatman talked on the way. Nasruddin was considered to be a very knowledgeable person. If knowledgeable people get a chance to prove that somebody else is ignorant, they don't miss it. Nasruddin asked the boatman, "Do you know how to read?"

The boatman said, "No, I know how to speak. I don't know anything about reading and writing."

Nasruddin said, "One-fourth of your life has been lost in futility, because if you don't know how to read how can you attain to any knowledge in your life? Idiot! How can anybody attain to knowledge without being able to read?" But the boatman started laughing silently....

Then they went a little further and Nasruddin asked, "Do you know anything about mathematics?"

The boatman said, "No, I don't know anything about mathematics at all. I just count on my fingers."

Nasruddin said, "Another fourth of your life has been lost in futility, because someone who does not know about mathematics, who cannot even calculate, cannot earn much of a living. How can he? In order to earn a living one needs to know how to count. But what can you earn? Half of your life has been futile."

Then a storm, a hurricane arose and the boat turned over and sank.

The boatman asked, "Can you swim?"

Nasruddin cried, "No, I can't swim!"

The boatman shouted, "Your whole life has been wasted. I am leaving. I don't know how to do mathematics or how to read a language, but I do know how to swim. So I am leaving you. Your whole life has gone to waste."

There are truths in life which can only be known by

the self; they cannot be known through books or through scriptures. The truth of the soul, or the truth of existence, can only be known by the self – there is no other way.

These things that are written in the scriptures – we can read them, we can understand them, we can memorize them, we can learn them, we can tell others about them – but no knowledge will be attained through them. The accumulation of facts and other people's opinions is not a sign of knowledge, it is only a sign of ignorance. A person who is conscious and awake is free of all this 'knowledge'. There is no question of him collecting any more facts – he knows himself. With that self-knowledge the mind is not a disturbed hive of honeybees; it is a mirror, a silent lake.

Your mind is a buzzing hive of thoughts which you have been breeding because you think they are knowledge. You have given them space in your house, you have made them residents. You have made your mind a caravanserai: whosoever comes can stay there as long as he is wearing the clothes of knowledge; then he has the right to stay. And the crowd in the caravanserai has increased and grown so much that it has become difficult to decide who is the master in this crowd. Those who are the guests are making such a noise that the one who shouts the most becomes the master – and you don't know who the real master is. Each thought shouts loudly that it is the master, so in this crowded caravanserai it has become impossible to know the real master.

No thought wants to leave. How can you get some-one to leave when you have invited him to stay? It is easy to invite a guest, but it is not so easy to get rid of him. For thousands of years these guests have been gathering in man's mind, and if I were to ask you to say goodbye to them today, you could not easily get rid of them.

But if you understand the nature of your illusions then it is possible to get rid of them. You cherish these thoughts because of your illusion that they are knowl-edge. So the first thing to understand is that all thoughts borrowed from others are futile. If this becomes clear to you, then you have cut the very root of your collection of thoughts and ideas: you have stopped giving water to the roots.

An old sage was passing through a jungle with one of his young monks. The night descended and it began to get dark. The old sage asked the young monk, "Son, do you think there is any danger along this path? This path leads through a dense forest, and it is getting dark. Is there anything to be afraid of?"

The young monk was very surprised because the question of being afraid should not arise in a san-nyasin. Whether the night was dark or bright, whether it was a forest or the marketplace, for a sannyasin to feel fear was very surprising. And this old man had never been afraid. What had happened today? Why was he afraid? Something or other was wrong.

They went on a little further and the night became

151

darker. The old man again asked, "Is there anything to worry about? Will we reach the next town soon? How far is it?" Then they stopped near a well to wash their hands and faces. The old man gave the bag on his shoulder to the young monk and said, "Take care of it."

The young man thought, "Certainly there must be something in the bag, otherwise there would be no question of fear or of taking care of it."

For a sannyasin even to take care of something was strange; then there is no point in becoming a sann-yasin, because a person who has things to take care of is a householder. What does a sannyasin need to take care of?

The old man started washing his face, so the young man put his hand inside the bag and saw a golden brick in the bag. Then he understood the cause of the fear. He threw the brick away in the forest and placed a stone of the same weight inside the bag. The old man returned quickly after washing his face, quickly took the bag, touched it, felt the weight, placed the bag on his shoulder and started walking again.

Then after walking for a little while he said, "It is be-coming very dark, have we forgotten the way? Is there any danger?"

The young man said, "Don't be afraid. I have thrown away the fear."

The old sage was shocked. He immediately looked into the bag and saw that, instead of the gold, there was a stone inside. For a moment he stood there stunned, then he started laughing and said, "I have been an idiot.

I have been carrying a stone, yet I was afraid because I thought it was a golden brick." When he realized that he had been carrying a stone, he threw it away and said to the young monk, "Tonight we will sleep here, because it is difficult to find the way in the dark." That night they slept peacefully in the forest.

If you think your thoughts and ideas are bricks of gold, you will take good care of them and stay very attached to them. But I want to say to you that they are not golden bricks, they are just heavy stones. What you think is knowledge is not knowledge at all; it is not gold, it is absolutely a stone.

The knowledge obtained from others is just a stone; only the knowledge that comes from within you is gold. The day you see that you are carrying a stone in your bag will be the day that the matter will be over. Then there will be no difficulty in throwing away the stone.

There is no difficulty in throwing away garbage, but there is difficulty in throwing away gold. As long as you feel that your thoughts are knowledge you cannot throw them away, and your mind will remain troubled. You may try thousands of ways to calm it, but nothing will work. Deep down you want the thoughts to remain because you think they are knowledge. The greatest difficulties in life arise from the misunderstanding that something is what it is not. Then all kinds of troubles arise. If somebody thinks that a stone is a brick of gold, then problems start. If somebody realizes that a stone is a stone, then the matter is over.

So the treasure of your thoughts is not a real treasure – this fact has to be understood. But how to understand it? Will you understand by my saying it is so? If you understand by my saying it, then this understanding will be a borrowed one; it will be futile. There is no question of your understanding something because I say it is so – you have to see, search and recognize for yourself.

If the young monk had said to the old man, "Keep walking. There is no need to worry. There is a stone in your bag, not gold" – it would still not have made any difference to the old man until he saw with his own eyes that this was the case. If the young man had simply told him, he would not have believed it. He would have just laughed at the young man and thought that he is just a boy, he is ignorant, he does not know anything. Or he could have believed him and accepted his words, but his acceptance would have been false – deep inside he would have still held on to the idea of keeping the gold brick safe. Only seeing it for himself made the difference.

So it is necessary to look into the bag of your mind to see if what you think is knowledge is really knowledge, or if you have just collected garbage. You have collected the sutras of the Gita, the statements of the Vedas, the words of Mahavira and Buddha, and you are continually remembering them, thinking about them and finding meanings in them. You keep on reading and writing commentaries on them, and discussing them with each other. Absolute madness has been created.

True knowledge has no relation to this madness. No flame, no light will arise in your life from this.

And by collecting this garbage you will create the illusion that you have attained a great wealth of knowledge, that you are a great master, that you have so much, that your vault is full – and you will live your life like this and destroy it.

A young monk was staying in a monastery. He had come to sit in the presence of an old sage, but within a few days he felt that the old man did not know anything at all. Listening to the same things every day, he got fed up. He thought that he should leave this monastery and search somewhere else for another master; this was not the place for him.

But on the day he was to leave, another monk visited the monastery. That night the residents of the monastery gathered and they talked about many things. The new monk was very knowledgeable about so many things, very subtle and perceptive, very deep and very intense, and the young monk thought that this was how a master should be. Within two hours the new monk had mesmerized everyone. The young monk thought that the old master must be feeling a lot of pain and feeling very depressed that he is so old and yet has not learned anything, while this newcomer knew so much.

After two hours, when the talks were over, the guest monk looked at the old master and asked, "How did you like my talks?"

The old man said, "*My* talks? You were talking, but

none of it was your own. I was listening very intently for you to say something, but you did not say anything at all."

The guest monk replied, "If it was not me talking, then who has been talking for the past two hours?"

The old man said, "If you ask for my truthful and authentic opinion, then books and scriptures were talking from inside you but you were not talking at all. You did not even say a single word. You were throwing out, vomiting whatever you have gathered. And because of your vomiting I have become afraid that you are a very sick person. For two hours you went on vomiting whatever was collected in your stomach, and you filled the whole room with the dirt and stink of it. I did not smell even a little fragrance of knowledge, because anything which is taken in from the outside and again thrown out is bound to have the stink of vomit. You did not say anything yourself – not a single word was your own."

After listening to the old sage, the young monk who had wanted to leave the monastery decided to stay. That day, for the first time, he realized that there are different kinds of knowledge.

One kind of knowledge is that which we collect from outside, and another kind, knowing, is that which arises from within. Whatever we collect from the outside becomes a bondage, it does not liberate us. We are liberated by that which comes from the inside.

So the first thing to look at inside is: do you really know whatever you know? It is necessary to question each thought and each word which you know: do you really know it? And if the answer is, "I do not know it," then all the golden bricks in your life will slowly turn into stones. It is possible to deceive everybody in the world, but it is not possible to deceive yourself.

No man can deceive himself. Whatever you do not know, you do not know. If I ask you, "Do you know truth?" and you nod your head and say, "Yes, I do," then you are not authentic. Ask yourself inside, "Do I know truth or have I just accepted the things which I have heard? And if I do not know, then this truth is not worth a single penny. How can something I do not know change my life? Only the truth I know can become a revolution in my life. Truth that I do not know is not worth a penny; it is false. And it is not truth at all; it is all borrowed and it is not going to change anything in my life."

It is as if I were to ask you, "Do you know about your soul?" and you would answer "Yes I do, because I have read about it in books, and the priest who teaches in our temple teaches that the soul exists." Man memorizes whatever is taught to him like a parrot, but this memorizing has nothing to do with knowing. If you are born in a Hindu family then you become one kind of parrot, if you are born in a Jaina family then you become another kind of parrot, and if you are born in a Mohammedan family then you become a third kind of parrot – but in each situation you become a parrot.

Whatever is taught to you, you go on repeating for your whole life. And because there are so many parrots around you, nobody objects, nobody argues. These other parrots nod their heads – "You are absolutely right" – because they have learned the same thing that you have learned. In religious meetings, the religious leaders are teaching and everybody is nodding their heads and agreeing that they are absolutely right because whatever the religious leaders have learned the people have also learned. And both groups are sitting there thinking that they have learned this too, and all are nodding their heads agreeing that, "Yes, what is being said is absolutely right. The same thing is written in our books also. We have also read the same thing."

The whole of humanity has been deceived about knowledge. This deception is a conspiracy against man. All this knowledge has to be cleaned out and thrown away – only then can you become open to the kind of knowing in the light of which existence is experienced and the flame of the soul is seen. This is not possible with pseudo-knowledge. Pseudo-knowledge is not light at all: the house is dark, the lamp is unlit – but people are convincing each other and explaining to each other that the lamp is lit. And after hearing it said again and again, you have also started saying that the lamp is lit. Because somewhere inside there is fear – others say that if you do not see the lighted lamp you will go to hell. They say they can see the lighted lamp, and so, slowly, slowly you start seeing it too.

There was once a great king. One morning a mysterious stranger came and said to him, "You have now conquered the whole earth, so the clothes of a human being do not suit you. I will bring you the clothes of the gods." The king's mind became greedy. His intellect was saying, "How can the gods have clothes?" The intellect is even doubtful about the existence of any gods. But he was greedy, because he thought that perhaps there were gods somewhere, and if their clothes were brought to him then he would be the first man on the earth, in the history of mankind, who has worn the clothes of a god. And in what way could this man deceive him? He was a great emperor, he had billions and trillions of rupees just lying around. Even if the man asked for several thousand rupees it would not matter. He asked the man, "Okay, so what will it cost?"

The man said, "It will cost at least ten million rupees, because in order to reach the gods I will have to pay a large bribe. Not only do men take bribes – the gods are also very clever, they also ask for bribes. And a man will agree to a small amount of money – he is poor – but the gods will not agree to a small amount. Only if it is a big pile of money will they look at it, otherwise they will not even look at it. So it is very difficult, but at least ten million rupees will be needed."

The king said, "Alright, that's no problem. But remember, if you deceive me then it will cost you your life. From today onwards there will be armed guards around your house."

The man was given ten million rupees and his house was put under guard. All the people in the neighborhood were surprised, amazed. They could not believe

159

this. They were thinking, "Where *are* the gods, and where *is* their heaven? This man does not seem to be coming or going anywhere." He stayed inside his house and told everybody, "After six months I will show you the clothes of the gods." Everybody was doubtful, but the king was unconcerned because the man was under a guard of naked swords. He could not escape, nor could he deceive.

But the man was much more intelligent than the king: after six months he came out of his house with a very beautiful box and said to the soldiers, "Let us go to the palace. Today is the day – the clothes have arrived."

The whole capital gathered. Kings and emperors from far away gathered to see. A great celebration was organized. The man had come into the court with the box, so there was no reason for any doubt. He brought the box and put it down. He opened the lid of the box, put his hand inside, brought out an empty hand and said to the king, "Take this turban." The king looked and said, "I cannot see any turban, your hand is empty."

Immediately the man said, "Let me remind you of one thing: the gods have said that only a person who is born of his own father will be able to see the turban and the clothes. Now do you see the turban?"

The king said, "Of course I can see it."

There was no turban there, the man's hand was empty – but all the courtiers started clapping. They too could not see the turban but they all started saying, "We have never seen such a beautiful turban. The turban is very beautiful, unique, wonderful. No man has ever seen such a turban."

When all the courtiers started saying that the turban was very beautiful, the king was in a difficult situation. And then the man said, "So now take off your turban and put this one on."

The king removed his own turban and put on the turban which did not exist. If it had only been a turban that was involved it would have been alright, but soon the king was really in trouble. First his coat was removed, then his shirt, and finally the time came when he had to remove his last garment. The king was now naked, but all the courtiers were shouting, "Such beautiful clothes! Wonderful! We have never seen such clothes." Every courtier had to say it very loudly in case other people might wonder if he was born of his own father or not.

And when the whole crowd was shouting about the clothes, each person was thinking that either something was wrong with his eyes or until now he had been mistaken about his father. "If all the other people are shouting about the clothes, they must be right. So many people cannot be wrong. There is such a majority. When everyone says the same thing it must be right." This is democracy: everybody is in agreement – "When so many people agree, they cannot all be wrong." So each person thought that he alone was wrong, and if he remained silent then people would think that he could not see.

The king became afraid – should he take off the last

article of clothing or not? On the one hand he was afraid that the whole court would see him naked, and on the other hand he was afraid that if the world came to know that he was not born of his father, then there would be even greater difficulties. It was like going from the devil to the deep blue sea! So in the end it seemed better to accept nudity; at least his father's name would be saved, his dynasty would not be defamed. He thought, "At the most, people might see me naked – so what. And also, when everybody is cheering about the clothes, they may be right. The clothes may really be there and it is only that I can't see them." So in order to avoid any unnecessary complications he dropped the last garment and stood there naked.

Then the man said, "Oh King! The clothes of the gods have descended on earth for the first time. You should have a procession and travel around the city on a chariot." The king became really afraid, but now there was no way out.

When man commits a mistake at the first stage then it becomes very difficult to stop at any later stage, and it becomes very difficult to return. If one is not honest at the first stage, then one keeps on getting more and more hypocritical at the next stages; it becomes difficult for him to know where to return from because each stage has become connected with many other stages.

So the king was in difficulty. He could not refuse. He was taken in a procession on a chariot.... Maybe you were also there, because there were many people in that city. Everyone saw the procession, so you might also have been there and you might have praised the clothes. Nobody would want to miss the chance. All the people were praising the clothes loudly, saying that they were very beautiful.

Only a child who was in the crowd sitting on his father's shoulders said, "Father, the king seems to be naked."

His father said, "You idiot, be quiet! You are small, you have no experience. When you become experienced you will also start seeing the clothes. *I* can see the clothes."

Children sometimes say the truth, but old people don't give them any credit because old people have more experience. And experience is a very dangerous thing. Because of his experience the father said, "Be quiet! When you become experienced you will also see the clothes. We can all see them – do you think we have all gone mad?"

Sometimes a child will say, "I cannot see God in a statue." Then old people say, "Be quiet! We can see God. Ram is standing there. And when you become experienced you will also see him."

Man is caught in a collective deception. And when everybody is caught in the same deception it becomes difficult to see.

You have to find out if the clothes of knowledge – which you have thought of as clothes – are really clothes, or are you standing naked in invisible clothes?

You have to test each of your thoughts according to this criterion: "Do I know this?" If you do not know, then be ready to go to hell rather than go on holding on to this pseudo-knowledge.

The first condition of authenticity is that whatever one does not know, one should say that one does not know it – otherwise it will be the beginning of hypocrisy. Usually we cannot see the big deceptions, we can only see small deceptions. If a man cheats you for a few rupees you notice it, but if a man stands with folded hands in front of a stone statue saying, "Oh God, oh Lord"... knowing very well that the statue is made of stone and that there is no God, no Lord there, then even though this man may seem to be authentic and religious, it would be difficult to find a greater deceiver or hypocrite on this earth. He is being absolutely deceptive. He is saying something absolutely false and he is not feeling anything inside himself. But he cannot gather enough courage to understand what he is saying, what he is doing.

A religious person is one who recognizes what he knows and does not know. This recognition is the first step towards becoming a religious person. A religious person is not one who says that he knows God and the soul, that he has seen heaven and hell. A religious person is one who says that he does not know anything, that he is absolutely ignorant: "I have no knowledge. I don't even know myself, so how can I say that I know existence? I don't even know the stone that is lying in front of my house. How can I say that I know the divine? Life is very mysterious, very unknown. I don't know anything. I am absolutely ignorant."

If you have the courage to be ignorant and the courage to accept that you are ignorant, then you can start on the path towards becoming free from the entanglement of your thoughts. Otherwise, you cannot even begin. So one thing needs to be understood: you are very ignorant, you don't know anything, and whatever you seem to know is absolutely false, borrowed and stale. It is like a pond, it is not like a well. If you want to create a well in your life, then it is very necessary to be free from the illusion of the pond.

And now, a question: *Your teachings are very similar to those of J. Krishnamurti. What is your opinion of him?*

I have no opinion. The first thing is that I don't know Krishnamurti.

The second point is that if when I am saying something, you compare it with someone else – who I am like, who I am not like – then you will not be able to listen to me. You will waste time in comparing.

It is absolutely impossible for there to be any similarity between the words of two persons, because two persons are not similar. Two leaves are not similar, two stones are not similar. There can be a similarity in some words, there may be a superficial similarity in something, but each and every person in the world is so different and so unique that nothing can be exactly the same.

If you start comparing what I am saying with the Gita or with Krishnamurti or with Ramakrishna or with Mahavira, you will not be able to listen to me because these Ramakrishnas, these Krishnamurtis and these Mahaviras will create so much trouble in between, that my words will not be able to reach you. There will be no direct relation between me and you.

So I don't know – but it is my suggestion that there is no need to compare and to find similarities. It is futile, pointless, and nobody is helped by it.

But some common habits have been formed in your lives, one of which is the habit of comparison. You cannot evaluate something without comparing it. If you want to evaluate something you cannot conceive how to do it without comparing – and whenever you compare the mistake begins.

If you compare a lily flower with a rose flower, then the mistake begins. A lily is a lily, a rose is a rose and a grass flower is a grass flower. The rose is neither higher than the grass flower nor lower. The grass flower lives in its uniqueness, a rose flower lives in its uniqueness. Neither is one lower or higher; neither is one equal or unequal. Everyone is like himself and not like anybody else. If this individuality of things, their personality, their uniqueness starts becoming apparent to you, only then you will stop comparing.

But you have the habit of comparing. You even compare small children with each other. You say, "Look, the other child has gone farther than you. You have been left behind." You are being unjust to the child because the other child is the other child and this child is this child. It is not possible to compare the two. Their beings are totally different, they are completely different. In their uniqueness, in their authenticity, they have no relation to each other.

You are in the habit of comparing. Your educational systems teach comparison, your systems of thought involve comparison. Without comparing, you cannot evaluate. And the result is that you do not understand anybody or any thought directly; many things stand in between.

So I will say only this much: I don't know how much similarity or dissimilarity there is between J. Krishnamurti and myself. I have not compared. And I ask you also not to compare – either me with somebody else, or anybody with anybody else.

This comparison goes on: how much similarity is there between Mahavira and Buddha, how much similarity is there between Christ and Mohammed, and how much similarity is there between Krishna and Rama? This is all stupid! There is no question of similarity or dissimilarity, because everyone is simply himself. The one has nothing to do with the other, the one has no relation with the other. It is absurd even to say 'dissimilarity' because if there is no similarity then there is no question of dissimilarity.

Everyone is unique, himself. In this world no two people are alike, no two events are repeated, no two experiences are repeated. There is nothing like repetition in life. Life goes on creating uniqueness continuously. So there is no need to compare or to evaluate. If you are listening to Krishnamurti, then you need to understand him directly. If you are listening to me, then you need to listen to me directly. If you are listening to your neighbor, then you need to listen to him directly. If you are listening to your wife, then you need to listen to her directly. If a third person comes in between, problems and quarrels begin. There is no need for a third person to come in between – our contact and communication should be direct and immediate.

If I am standing in front of a rose flower, and if I remember the flowers that I saw yesterday, and if I start thinking of how much similarity there is between this flower and those flowers, then my seeing this flower will stop. One thing is certain: the shadow of those flowers which come in between will not let me see *this* flower. And if I want to see the flower which is in front of me, then I need to forget all the flowers which I have ever seen. To bring them in between will be unjust to this flower. And there is also no need to carry the memory of this flower, otherwise tomorrow, looking at some other flower, this one may come in between.

So don't bring Krishnamurti here. And don't think that because you are listening to me you can bring me in between while you listen to someone else, because it will be unjust to that person.

See life directly. There is no need to bring anybody in between. Nobody is equal or unequal; everybody is simply like himself. And I would like everybody to become just himself.

Everybody should be himself: this is what I see as the fundamental rule of life. But until now you have not been able to accept it. Until now mankind has not been ready to accept each individual as he is – you try to make him become like somebody else: he should become like Mahavira, like Buddha, like Gandhi. This is a direct insult to the individuality of each person.

When you say to a person, "Become like Gandhi," you have greatly insulted him because he was not born to become a Gandhi. One Gandhi has already been born, what is the use of another one? To tell this man to become like Gandhi is to say that he has no right to be himself; he only has the right to be a copy of someone else, to imitate someone else. He can only be a carbon copy, he cannot be an original. This is an insult to this man.

So I do not say that everyone should become like everybody else, I only say that everyone should become himself. Then this world can become a wonderful and beautiful world. Until now we have only tried to organize things so that everyone becomes like everybody else. That is why you compare, you think, you search. There is no need to do this. It is absolutely unnecessary to think in such a way.

If there are any more questions in this context, we will talk about them tonight. Let me repeat again – I have told you only one thing, one very fundamental thing: look at your knowledge and decide if it is your own or someone else's. If you see that it belongs to somebody else then it is futile. But the day you see that you do not have any knowledge of your own, from that very moment the light of your own knowledge will begin to arise from within. From that very moment, the revolution will begin.

If there are any more questions we will talk about them tonight. The afternoon meeting is over.

NO BELIEF, NO DISBELIEF

CHAPTER SIX

NO BELIEF, NO DISBELIEF

M Y   B E L O V E D   O N E S ,

Man is tied up in chains of thoughts, like a prisoner. In this prison of thoughts, what kinds of stones have been used as a foundation? In the afternoon we talked about one of those stones; tonight we will talk about the second, but equally important, one. If these two foundation stones are removed, the mistake of thinking that borrowed knowledge is real knowledge can be seen, and man will then very easily be able to rise above his prison of thoughts.

What is this second stone? What is the other foundation stone on which the prison of thoughts in man's mind has been built, on which the web of thoughts has been woven? Perhaps you do not know. Perhaps you have no idea how you have become so full of so many contradictory thoughts.

Your situation is like a bullock cart which is being pulled by bullocks from all four sides: the bullocks are being forced to move so that different destinations can be reached; the bullock cart is in danger, its structure is becoming loose; the bullocks are pulling it in different directions from all sides. Can it go anywhere? Can it reach any destination? There can be only one destination for it, only one destiny: it will be broken apart, destroyed. With the bullocks pulling it apart, running away in opposite directions with all its pieces, nothing but destruction can happen. The bullock cart cannot reach anywhere.

The inner conflict between the different thoughts in your mind is killing you. All your thoughts are irrelevant and contradictory, in opposition to each other. All the bullocks of your thoughts are pulling the mind in different directions, and you are in misery and suffering in the middle of this. You have no idea how this struggle, this conflict, has come to be there within you.

I was a guest in the house of a very great doctor. In the morning the doctor and I were about to go out of the house when suddenly his child sneezed. The doctor said, "This means bad luck! Let's wait for awhile, for a few minutes, and then we will go."

I said, "You seem to be a strange doctor. At least a doctor should know what causes a sneeze, and that there is no relation between sneezing and whether somebody should stay or go somewhere. This is just a superstition. It is very surprising that even a doctor isn't clear about this."

I told the doctor that even if I became sick and was close to death, I would not be treated by him. In my opinion, his doctor's certificate should be taken away – it was wrong for him to have one. It was very surprising that because of a childhood superstition, he would not go somewhere when somebody sneezed. The ideas acquired in childhood were still working even though the man had become a doctor, an FRCS from London. Two thoughts were present in him at the same time: when somebody sneezed his feet would stop, and yet at the same time he knew very well that it was absolutely stupid, that there was no relation between the two. Both thoughts together and functioned in his mind at the same time.

Thousands of these types of thoughts exist within you, and they are all pulling you in different directions at the same time. You have become very disturbed, that much is obvious. This is why man seems to be absolutely mad. What else can he be? Madness is an obvious consequence. An infinite number of contradictory thoughts from thousands and thousands of years have gathered in the mind of one man. Thousands of generations, thousands of centuries, are living in one person at the same time. A five-thousand-year-old thought and an ultramodern thought from the present time exist simultaneously within him, and there can be no comparison or any harmony between these two thoughts.

Thoughts coming from thousands of different directions have collected within one man. The ideas of thousands of *tirthankaras* and *digambaras*, *avataras* and gurus are residing within him, and all of them have done a unique thing: although they have not agreed on anything else, all the religions, all the teachers, all the preachers of the world have always agreed on one strategy, and that is to tell people to believe in what they are saying. All of them say, "Believe in what we are saying" – they disagree on everything else. A Hindu says one thing, a Mohammedan says something, a Jaina says yet another thing and a Christian says something else, but on this one point they all agree: "Believe in what we say." All of them say contradictory things and all their contradictory sayings land on man's being, and all of them shout at him to believe in what they are saying. Man is weak: he believes whatsoever all these people say. They all laugh at each other's words, but nobody laughs at their own stupidities.

Christians say that Jesus was born out of a virgin girl and that someone who does not accept this will go to hell. The poor listener feels afraid: if he does not accept this point he will go to hell, so he accepts that what these people say is right. What does it matter if a virgin girl gave birth to Jesus or not? There is no need to go to hell over such a point.

The rest of the people of the world laugh at this Christian idea. Mohammedans, Jainas, Hindus laugh at this stupidity. How can a child be born out of a virgin girl? It is absolutely absurd.

But Mohammedans say that while in his body, Mohammed went to heaven sitting on his female horse. Christians, Hindus, Jainas laugh at this – what kind of stupidity is this? The first thing is that a female horse cannot go to heaven. At least if it had been a male horse it might have been able to go. A man can go to heaven, but there is no provision for women to go, so a female horse cannot go to heaven. If it had been a male horse the idea might have been tolerated, it might have been alright.

And secondly, how can somebody go to heaven while still alive in his body? The body has to be left here, the body is a thing of the earth. Mohammed cannot go to heaven in his body. Everybody laughs at the idea. Christians, Jainas and Hindus all laugh, but Mohammedans say, "Believe it! If you don't believe it then you will go to hell. You will be forced to rot in hell, you will suffer in hell. You will have to accept this. If you do not accept it, if you do not agree with Mohammed's words, then know well that you will get into great difficulty – because there is only one God in the world and Mohammed is his prophet."

Man is under a threat to believe, so he accepts that what he is told may be right. Jainas laugh at Mohammedans and Christians, but they themselves say that Mahavira was conceived in a *brahmin* woman's womb. And how can a Jaina tirthankara be born in a brahmin family? The real and the highest is the *kshatriya* caste, the warrior cast, so tirthankaras are always born in kshatriya families; they cannot be born in brahmin houses. Brahmins are beggars – how could a tirthankara have been born in such a house? So Mahavira was conceived in a brahmin woman's womb, but when the gods saw that this was going to be a great mistake – "How can a tirthankara be born in a brahmin family?" – they immediately removed the embryo and placed it in the womb of a kshatriya woman, and they took out the female embryo from the kshatriya woman's womb and put it in the brahmin woman's womb.

People all over the world laugh at all these things – they are very funny! First of all, what have gods to do with changing the embryo in somebody's womb? How can this happen? The whole world laughs, but then Jainas become angry. They say, "You can laugh at this, but you don't know what our tirthankara has said, and whatever has been said by our tirthankara is absolutely true. Whosoever does not believe this will suffer in hell. If you do not believe it we are not concerned, you can suffer!"

Man is asked to believe many things by many people. There was a time when he did not know everyone's beliefs. People were living in their own circles: they only knew things within their own circle so there was not so much confusion. Now the world has become very small and everybody knows everyone else's beliefs, so man's confusion has reached a point of absolute madness! Now it is beyond his understanding what all this noise is about, what it is that people are trying to convince him about.

But even in the past, the situation was not much better. A Hindu not knowing about Mohammedan beliefs or a Jaina not knowing about Christian beliefs did not make the situation any clearer. Even Jainas themselves do not believe in essentially the same things: the *digambaras* say one thing, the *svetambaras* say something else. You would be very surprised to know which things they disagree about. It is amazing that people can have such different opinions about such things. One of the twenty-four Jaina tirthankaras was Mallinath. The digambaras say that he was a man and the svetambaras say that he was a woman. The svetambaras say that she was Mallibai, the digambaras say that he was Mallinath – and both of them say, "If you don't believe us you will go to hell!" Digambaras say that a woman could never have been a tirthankara – the fact itself is false – so he must have been a man. He was Mallinath, not Mallibai. It is really too much to have a conflict over whether a person is a man or a woman. But man is threatened that if he does not believe he will go to hell and will have to suffer, so he had better believe it.

All over the world, the teachings of the people who want you to believe them have created a chaos and a confusion in your mind. You listen to everybody and the impressions of all their teachings remain within you, and your being is pulled in many different directions.

And then, after all these religions, came communism. Communism said that religion is just like opium: there is no meaning in it, the idea of God is absolutely false, it is all meaningless. Marx says communism is the real religion; one should believe in it and nothing else. The Bible, the Gita, the Koran are all wrong – *Das Kapital* is the real religious scripture and one should believe only in it. So a new belief began....

Then, after communism came science. Science said that all these things are meaningless. Whatever is written in the religious scriptures is all wrong, only what science says is right. And even during the life of one scientist, another scientist has a different idea and claims that he is right and that the first man is wrong. Then along comes a third scientist who claims that he is right and the previous two are wrong. And then perhaps a fourth scientist....

These proclaimers of truth have created a confused

entanglement of thoughts in the mind and psyche of man, thoughts which are very different and pull man in all directions. Fear and manipulation have been used to create this entanglement; subtle methods of fear and manipulation have been used to impose a set of beliefs on man: if you believe you go to heaven, if you don't believe you go to hell.

These religious leaders have been doing the same thing that today's advertising is doing, but advertising is not as bold or as courageous. The people selling Lux toilet soap advertise that a certain beauty queen says, "I became beautiful because I used Lux toilet soap," so whoever uses it will become beautiful and whoever does not use it will not become beautiful. Then you become afraid that you may become ugly, so you go out and buy Lux toilet soap. As if people were not beautiful before there was Lux toilet soap; as if Cleopatra, Mumtaj and Noorjehan were not beautiful because there was no Lux toilet soap. But the advertisers are not really courageous yet: perhaps in the future they will say, "A certain tirthankara says, a certain prophet says, a certain teacher says that someone who does not use Lux toilet soap will go to hell, he cannot go to heaven. Only those people who use Lux toilet soap can go to heaven."

People can be threatened that only if they smoke Havana cigars will they go to heaven, because to smoke and to get others to smoke Havana cigars is a very good thing. And anyone who does not smoke Havana cigars will have to go to hell. And if he smokes Indian *bidis*, he will have to suffer eternal hell! If somebody does not believe all this then he will have to face the consequences: anyone who believes it will have good consequences and anyone who does not believe will have bad consequences.

Modern advertising has not yet become as bold as the old advertising was. The old advertising threatened man by telling him absolutely false things, and he went on listening to those things and accepting them without question. In fact, any untruth, if it is repeated many times for thousands of years, starts to look like the truth. If somebody goes on repeating even the most untrue thing – goes on repeating and repeating it – slowly, slowly you will start thinking that perhaps it may be true; otherwise how could it have been repeated so many times and for so long?

A poor farmer from a village bought a baby goat in the city. As he started walking towards his village with the baby goat, a few of the city hooligans thought that if they could somehow manage to get the baby goat, they would be able to enjoy a good meal and also a celebration. They could invite some friends and have a feast. But how to get hold of it?

The illiterate villager seemed to be a very strong and healthy man, and the hooligans of the city were weak and unhealthy. To take the goat directly from the farmer could lead to a fight and there could be trouble, so they had to be very careful and somehow trick him. They decided on a trick.

When the villager was about to leave the city, one of

the four or five hooligans met him on the road and said, "Hello. Good morning."

He replied, "Good morning."

Then the hooligan looked up and said, "Why are you carrying this dog on your shoulders?" – in fact, he was carrying the baby goat on his shoulders – "Where did you buy this dog? It is a very good dog."

The farmer laughed. He said, "Have you gone mad? It is not a dog! I have bought a goat, it is a baby goat."

The man said, "Don't go to your village carrying a dog, otherwise people will think you are mad. Do you really think this is a goat?" And the man went on his way.

The farmer laughed and thought that this was very strange, but he touched the goat's legs to see whether it was a goat or a dog...that had been the hooligan's motive. The farmer found that it really was a goat, and feeling reassured he went on walking.

In the next street the second hooligan met him. He said, "Hello, you have bought a very good dog. I also want to buy a dog. Where did you buy it?" Now the villager could not say with the same confidence that this was not a dog, because now a second man was saying the same thing, and two people cannot be mistaken.

Still he laughed and said, "This is not a dog, sir, it is a goat."

The man said, "Who told you that it is a goat? It seems that somebody has cheated you. What kind of goat is this?" And he went away.

The villager took the goat down from his shoulders to

see what was the matter, but it was definitely a goat – both of those people were mistaken. But he became afraid that perhaps he was suffering from a delusion.

Now he felt a bit afraid as he continued walking down the road when he met the third person who said, "Hello. Where did you buy this dog?" This time he did not have the courage to say that this was a goat. He answered, "I bought it in the city." It was very difficult for him to say that it was a goat, and he started to think that maybe he should not take it to his village: he had wasted the money and he would be laughed at in his village; people would think that he had gone mad.

While he was thinking this, the fourth man met him, and said, "This is strange – I have never seen anybody carrying a dog on his shoulders. Do you imagine that this is a goat?"

The villager looked around and saw that he was alone, nobody was around, so he dropped the goat and ran quickly to his village. His five rupees had been wasted, but at least he would not be called mad.

And the four hooligans took the goat with them.

Because four people repeated something again and again, it became difficult for the farmer to believe that what they were saying could be wrong. And when the people who are telling you something are dressed in religious clothing, it becomes even more difficult. And when these people are the so-called models of truth and sincerity, it becomes still more difficult. And when they are sincere renouncers of the world, it becomes much more difficult, because there is no reason to disbelieve what they are saying. It is not that they are necessarily deceiving you: ninety-nine times out of a hundred, they are people who have a wrong conception themselves and they themselves have been deceived. It need not be that they are deceivers, but they are in the same rut as you are.

One thing is certain: as long as man continues to believe, he will continue to be exploited. As long as man is asked to believe, he will not become free from exploitation. Then the belief may be of a Hindu or a Jaina or a Mohammedan, or of anybody else; it may be of a communist or a non-communist, whatever, but as long as man is told to believe what others are saying and is told that, "If you don't believe you will suffer, and if you do believe you will be happy"; as long as this trick is used it will be very difficult for man to gather enough courage to be rid of the entanglement of thoughts within him.

What do I want to tell you? I want to tell you that if you want to get rid of the entanglement of thoughts which has been formed within you – to which thousands of centuries have contributed, in which impressions of hundreds of years are collected – then one thing must be fully understood: there is nothing more suicidal than belief. One thing you have to definitely understand is that to believe, to believe blindly, to accept silently with closed eyes, has been the basic reason why your lives have been crippled until now.

But everybody asks you to believe them; they tell

you to believe them and not to believe others. They say, "Do not believe other people because they are wrong. I am right, believe me."

I want to tell you that it is destructive to believe anybody, and it will be harmful to your life. No belief, no belief at all! Whosoever makes a belief system a basis for his life is entering into a world of blindness – and no light can ever enter into his life. He can never attain to light in his life. Someone who believes in others will never be able to know himself.

So am I asking you to disbelieve? No, there is no need to disbelieve either. But you think that if you don't believe in something, then you inevitably disbelieve in it. This is an absolutely wrong idea. There is a state of mind which neither believes nor disbelieves.... Disbelief is a form of belief. When you say that you don't believe in God, what are you saying? You are saying that you believe in the non-existence of God. When you say, "I don't believe in the soul," then you are saying that you believe in the non-existence of the soul. Belief and disbelief are similar things, there is no difference between them. Belief is positive and disbelief is negative. Belief is a positive faith and disbelief is a negative faith – but both are faiths.

A person can become free from his inner entanglement of thoughts only if he becomes free of this faith and belief, if he becomes free of continually looking towards others for their point of view, if he drops the very idea that anybody else can give him truth. As long as a person has the idea that someone else can give him truth he will be in bondage in some way or other. If he gets free from one he will be tied to another, if he gets free from the second he will be tied to the third – he cannot get free from the bondage. But to get free of one and to be tied to the other always gives consolation for awhile.

When a man dies, four people carry his dead body to the funeral ground on a bier on their shoulders; when one shoulder starts aching they change to the other shoulder. For a while they get relief for the tired shoulder, then the second shoulder gets tired and they change to the other shoulder again. A person who changes his beliefs is only changing from one shoulder to the other; but the weight is always present, it makes no difference. One gets relief only for awhile.

If a Hindu becomes a Mohammedan, if a Mohammedan becomes a Jaina, if a Jaina becomes a Christian; if someone drops all religions and becomes a communist or something else, if he is just dropping one belief system and grabbing hold of another, there will be no change in the burden on his mind. He will get relief for awhile but it is only a change in the weight on his shoulders. There is no significance in that kind of relief.

I have heard that there were two men in a village, one a theist, an extreme theist, and one an atheist, an extreme atheist. The whole village was very troubled because of the two of them. Villages always get into difficulty because of such people. Day and night the theist was explaining about the existence of God, and

day and night the atheist was refuting it. The people of
the village were in great difficulty about who to follow
and who not to follow. At last they decided that, since
they were so troubled, both men should be told to debate between themselves in front of the whole village.
And the village people said, "We will follow the one
who wins. Don't make difficulties for us. You must debate with each other, and we will follow whoever wins."

One night, on a full-moon night, the debate was
arranged in the village. The whole village gathered.
The theist explained the theories of theism, presented
all his arguments and refuted atheism. Then the atheist
refuted theism and gave all his arguments in favor of
atheism. The debate went on the whole night, and in
the morning the result was that the theist had become
an atheist and the atheist had become a theist. Each
had liked the other's arguments.

But the problem for the villagers remained, it was not
solved. The two men had convinced each other so
thoroughly, that both became converted. So there was
still an atheist and a theist in the village, the sum total
remained the same – and the problem for the village
remained the same as well.

If you change one belief for another belief it will
make no difference to your life. The problem for your
being will remain the same, there will be no difference.
The problem for your being has nothing to do with
being a Hindu or a Mohammedan, a Jaina, a Christian,
a communist or a fascist – the problem for your being

is that you believe. As long as you believe, you put yourself in bondage, you put yourself in prison and you are tied in some way or other, somewhere or other.

How can an imprisoned person, an imprisoned mind, become free from thoughts? How can he become free from the thoughts which he is holding on to with his whole being and which he believes in? How can he get rid of them? It is very difficult. You can get rid of them only if you remove the foundation stone.

Belief is the foundation stone at the bottom of the pile of thoughts. Man has learned to think on the basis of belief, and when thoughts grip the mind tightly, a fear also takes hold: "What will happen if I drop them?" So man says that if he is given something better to hold on to, only then he can drop his present thoughts – but the idea of dropping the very idea of holding on does not enter his mind.

Freedom, liberation of the mind, happens not from changing one's beliefs but from becoming free from belief itself.

Buddha was visiting a small village. Some people brought a blind man to him and said, "This man is blind and we are his closest friends. Although we try in every way to convince him that there is light, he is not ready to accept the fact. His arguments are such that we are at a loss. Even though we know that there is light, we have to admit defeat. The man tells us that he wants to touch light. Now how do we make it possible for him to touch light? Then the man says, 'Okay, if it cannot be touched then I want to hear it. I have ears – make the sound of light so that I can hear it. If this is also not possible then I want to taste it, or if the light has a fragrance I want to smell it.'"

There is no way to convince the man. Light can only be seen if one has eyes – and he had no eyes. He complained to the village people that they were unnecessarily talking about light just to prove that he was blind. He felt that they had invented the story of light just to prove him blind.

So the people asked Buddha if, as he was in the village for awhile, perhaps he could make their blind man understand.

Buddha said, "I am not insane enough to try to convince him. Mankind's problems have been created by people who have tried to explain things to those who cannot see. Preachers are a plague to humanity – they tell people things which they cannot understand."

So he said, "I won't make this mistake. I will not explain to this blind man that there is light. You have brought him to the wrong person. There was no need to bring him to me, take him instead to a physician who can treat his eyes. He does not need preaching, he needs treatment. This is not a question of explanations or of him believing in things you tell him – it is a question of treating his eyes. If his eyes are cured there will be no need for you to explain – he himself will be able to see, he himself will be able to know."

Buddha was saying that he did not consider religion to be just a philosophical teaching: it should be a practical cure. So he recommended that the blind man be taken to a physician.

The villagers liked what Buddha said so they took the blind man to a physician for treatment, and fortunately after a few months he was cured. By that time Buddha had gone to another village, so the blind man followed him. He bowed to Buddha, touched his feet and said, "I was wrong. There is such a thing as light, but I couldn't see it."

Buddha answered, "You were certainly wrong. But your eyes were cured because you refused to believe what others told you unless you experienced it for yourself. If you had accepted what your friends had told you, then the matter would have ended there and no question of treatment for your eyes would have arisen."

People who believe are unable to reach any understanding. People who accept silently are unable to have any experience of their own. The journey of those who are blind and hold on to the fact that if the others say that there is light, then certainly there must be light, ends right there. The journey only continues when your restlessness stays and stays and stays and never disappears. Restlessness comes only when you feel that there is something which people say is there, but you don't see it and so you cannot accept it. You can accept it only when you see it. This kind of restlessness that says, "I will accept only when I see with my own eyes," needs to be there in the mind.

The people who want you to have beliefs are the

ones that say that you don't need eyes of your own: "Mahavir had eyes, that is enough; Buddha had eyes, that is enough. Why should everybody need eyes? Krishna had eyes and wrote the Gita, then why do you need eyes? Read the Gita and enjoy it. Krishna could see, and he described what he could see, so what is the need for everyone to see? You should simply believe. Those who could see have already spoken – your job is simply to believe. The knowledge has been attained, what is the need for you to know for yourself?"

This teaching has kept man blind. Most of the people on earth have remained blind, and today most of them are still blind. And looking at the situation now, most people will probably stay blind in the future as well because the basic alchemy to correct the blindness – which is the thirst to overcome the blindness – has been killed. It has been destroyed by supplying strong belief systems.

In fact it should be said that however good Krishna's eyes were and however far they could see, they are not your eyes. And however beautiful Mahavira's eyes were – just like a lotus – they are not your eyes. Your eyes may not be very significant – they may be only like a field flower, not a lotus, but they are your own eyes. And you can see only with your own eyes.

So you should search for your own understanding, because you cannot attain to anything by worshipping the insights of another. In fact, the search for your own understanding can only begin when you drop the ideas of others. As long as there is any outer substitute, as long as something is being supplied from the outside, the search cannot begin.

When there is no support or fulfillment from somewhere else, when nothing can be attained from anyone else, then a challenge arises within you to search for your own way, for your own understanding.

Man is very lazy. If he can attain to knowledge without making any effort, why should he make the effort, why should he do any work? If enlightenment can be attained just by believing, without seeking, then why should he try to make the journey to enlightenment on his own? And when someone says, "Believe in me, I will take you to enlightenment," why should he make a huge effort by himself? When somebody says, "Sit in my boat. I will take you to the other shore and then the matter is over," he would rather sit silently in the boat and go to sleep.

But no one can reach anywhere in somebody else's boat. And no one can see with another's eyes – no one ever has and no one ever will. You have to walk on your own feet, you have to see with your own eyes, you have to live by your own heartbeat. You have to live and you have to die alone. No one can live in another's place and no one can die in another's place. You cannot take another's place, nor can someone else take your place. If there is one thing that is utterly impossible in this world, it is the notion that anyone can take anyone else's place.

Two soldiers were lying in a battlefield during the

second world war. One soldier was about to die. He was so badly wounded that there was obviously no hope for him. The other soldier was also wounded, but he was alive and there was no question of his dying. They were friends.

The dying soldier hugged his friend and said, "Now I must say goodbye to you because there is no possibility of my surviving. I suggest one thing: take my record book and give your record book to me. Your record book is not good, there are many humiliating comments in your record book. But my record is good, so let's exchange our books. This way the officers will think that you have died and I am alive. Because my record is good, you will be able to get a good promotion and you will get more respect. So hurry! Let's exchange the book and the number."

The dying friend's wish was absolutely right, because soldiers only have numbers, they have no names. And a soldier has only a record book, no soul. So it was right that they should exchange books – a bad man would die and a good man would remain alive.

But the man who was not going to die answered, "Forgive me. I can take your book and your number, but I will still be myself. I am a bad man and I will remain a bad man. I drink alcohol – I will still drink it. I go to prostitutes – I will still go to them. How long will your good record book remain good? How long can a book deceive anyone? On the contrary, two people will become bad. You will die as a bad man, but a bad man will still be alive. Now at least people will say that a good man has died. They will offer you flowers – if you were me they would not offer flowers. You cannot be in my place and I cannot be in your place. Your idea about changing places comes from your love for me, and it is good, but this is against the laws of life.

Nobody can change places with another. Nobody can live or die in place of another. You cannot know on behalf of another, neither can you have the ability to see on behalf of another.

The people who want you to have beliefs have told you to look through somebody else's eyes: "Look through the eyes of the tirthankaras, look through the eyes of the avataras." And you have continued to believe, which is why you have got entangled in a net. Thousands of teachers have created so much noise, and the followers of the thousands of teachers have made so much noise, that they have created a great fear of hell and a great greed for heaven...so slowly, slowly you have accepted what they say. And the words of all of them have created such a chaos within you that the journey of your life will be disrupted before it can go anywhere.

So the first thing for an intelligent person to do is to say goodbye to all his contradictory thoughts and decide, "I will not believe. I want to know. The day that I understand for myself, only on that day will I be able to use the word 'belief'. Before that there can be nothing like belief for me. It is deception, it is self-deception. I cannot deceive myself and say that I know without knowing, that I recognize without recognizing. It is not possible for me to accept blindly."

This does not mean that you are rejecting something; it simply means that you are standing aloof from both acceptance and rejection. You are saying, "I neither agree nor disagree. I neither say that Mahavira is wrong nor do I say that he is right. I simply say that I do not know myself what Mahavira is saying, so I have no right to agree or disagree. The day I come to know for myself that he is right, I will agree. If I come to know that what he says is wrong, then I will disagree. But I do not know yet, so how can I say yes or no?"

If your mind could distance itself from both acceptance and rejection, then the entanglement could break here and now. If the basic substance of this net is broken, then it will be as fragile as a house of cards which falls down with a little push. Right now it is like a stone castle with a solid foundation of stones set so deeply that they cannot easily be seen. So your mind is conditioned to understand that the people who believe and accept are religious, and those who reject and do not believe are irreligious.

But I say unto you that the person who believes is not religious, nor is one who disbelieves. A religious person is one who is true. 'True' means that he neither believes nor disbelieves what he does not know. He simply announces, with utter sincerity, that he does not know, that he is ignorant, so there is no question at all of his acceptance or rejection.

Can you gather the courage and strength to take

your being to this middle point? If you can, then this castle of thoughts will immediately collapse – there is no difficulty in it at all.

I told you three points this morning, one point this afternoon, and one now. Think about these five points carefully. Don't start using them just because I have talked about them, otherwise I will also become a preacher for you. Don't believe something just because I have said it – because maybe what I have said is all wrong, maybe it is false, meaningless, so you may get into difficulty. Don't believe what I have said.

Think, search and see, and if through your own experience you feel that there is some truth in what I say, if you feel because of your own search, because of looking into the window of your own mind, that there is some truth in it, then that truth will become a truth of your own. Then it will not remain only mine. Then it is not my understanding, it becomes an understanding of your own. Then whatever you do will become a way for your life to move towards wisdom and awakening. But whatever you do through believing will take you into more darkness and unconsciousness. It is helpful to think carefully about this point also.

Before we sit for the night meditation, I will answer some questions which have been asked about meditation. First I will talk about them, and then we will sit for the meditation.

A friend has asked if chanting, chanting some sacred mantra, can be helpful in meditation.

It cannot be helpful at all. On the contrary, it can

become an obstacle, because when you chant a mantra you repeat the same thought again and again. A mantra is a thought. When you chant a name, you repeat the same word again and again. A word is a part of a thought, a piece of a thought. So if you want to become free of thoughts by repeating a thought, you are making a mistake. As long as you go on repeating one thought it will seem that there are no other thoughts in your mind because, as I told you, the nature of the mind is to be stuck on a single thought. But the thought which you are repeating is as much a thought as other thoughts are; there is nothing useful in repeating it. On the contrary, it is harmful because by repeating the same word again and again, an unconsciousness, a sleep is created in the mind.

Take any one word and repeat it again and again – soon sleep will arise within you, not wakefulness. The repetition of any word is a way to create sleep. So if you cannot sleep it will be helpful to repeat 'Rama, Rama' or 'om, om' at night, but it will not be helpful in your search for the realization of the self, for truth, for a deeper realization of existence.

This method is known to everybody in every village, but you have never thought about it. When a mother wants her child to go to sleep she says, "Go to sleep, my little darling...go to sleep, little darling...go to sleep little darling...". She is using a mantra. She is repeating the same two words: little darling, little darling, "Go to to sleep, little darling, go to sleep, little darling. After awhile the little darling will definitely go to sleep. If the mother thinks that the child has gone to sleep because of her very musical voice, then she is making a big mistake: the child goes to sleep out of boredom. If you sit at somebody's head and say, "Go to sleep little darling, go to sleep little darling," he will get bored. The small child cannot run away anywhere, so the only way to escape is to go to sleep so that he can no longer hear this nonsense. The only way to get rid of this nonsense, the only escape, is to go to sleep; otherwise he will have to listen to this, "Go to sleep little darling, go to sleep little one." How long will the little darling be ready to listen to this nonsense? Howsoever darling the little one may be, he will also start feeling tired, and in that tiredness, in that boredom, the only alternative he has is to quickly go to sleep; only then will the nonsense stop.

So if you go on repeating 'little darling, little darling' or 'Ram, Ram' – it does not make any difference which word you use, they are all the same – then you have started doing the same thing to your mind that the mother is doing to the little child. So after a time the mind will become tired, bored, fed up, and then there is only one way to escape: it goes to sleep to avoid the nonsense. If you think this going to sleep is meditation, you are making a great mistake. This sleep is a state of unconsciousness. Yes, you will feel good after it. After this sleep you will feel as good as after every sleep. You will feel some relief because for that time you have escaped from worry, pain, from life itself.

It is the same kind of feeling that an alcoholic, a drug

addict or an opium user has as long as he is intoxicated. He forgets all his worries, until he regains consciousness and finds that the pain is still there – then he needs more opium. At first, only a little portion of opium was enough, but then after a few days he needs double the amount, and after a few more days even more than that.

There are *sadhus* who have used so much opium, that after awhile opium stops having any effect. So they breed snakes, and only when they get the snakes to bite their tongues can they become intoxicated, otherwise nothing happens.

With intoxicants, a person always needs more and more intoxicants, so if today he chants 'Ram, Ram' for fifteen minutes, then tomorrow he will need thirty minutes. After a month he will need an hour. Then he will need two hours, then ten hours.... Then he cannot run his shop because he needs to chant 'Ram, Ram' before starting work. So he has to go into the forest and drop everything because this Ram-chant has become an addiction. And now the more often he does it, the more important it will seem, because if he comes out of it he will feel pain. Then he says that now he will chant for twenty-four hours a day, but this is touching the boundaries of madness.

No knowledge, no understanding can arise in a man's life from this. And the countries and nations that get caught up in this kind of madness lose everything and become spiritless. India is a clear and living example: it has lost all its life, glory and spirit. It has become spiritless because of these kinds of stupidities. Glory does not develop through repetition; repetition gives birth only to unconsciousness.

So the cultures which have understood the method of repetition, which have learned to go to sleep by repeating something.... If your child is sick at home, you can avoid the situation by chanting 'Ram, Ram'. As you become unconscious the child disappears, the world disappears, you do not know anything anymore. If you cannot find a job you chant 'Ram, Ram' and avoid the situation. Now you don't need to worry about a job or food. The poor and needy countries go on finding these kinds of ways to avoid doing something constructive, and in this way they go on becoming more and more poor and destitute.

Life changes through fight and struggle. Life changes through the effort of facing it and changing it. Life does not change by keeping your eyes closed and chanting mantras. All these things are simply opium, so forget about chanting words, names, mantras.

Meditation is the way for waking up the consciousness deep inside you, not making it go to sleep. That which is hiding deep inside you should wake up and become so aware that not a single part inside remains asleep. Your whole being should wake up. Meditation is the name of that state of awareness.

But in India you can lie there in an unconscious state, and the people around you will say that you have attained to *samadhi*. Saliva can be dribbling out of your mouth and you might be lying there dizzy, in a fit, and people will say that you have attained to samadhi. This is hysteria, but people think that you are in samadhi. This is neither meditation nor samadhi – it is just a hysterical disease. Becoming unconscious is a disease. In America or Europe, if somebody becomes hysterical or falls sick he is treated, but in India people are so mad and ignorant that they will sing devotional songs around the person, saying that this great man has attained samadhi. If they were intelligent they would arrange for some treatment for all these great people. They are all sick, not healthy. Their disease is mental; it is the ultimate result of mental tension. It is not samadhi when a person is lying on the ground unconscious with saliva dribbling out of his mouth. It is sheer stupidity that the devotees are singing songs and saying that the person has attained to samadhi. Samadhi means total awareness, it does not mean sleep or unconsciousness.

Samadhi means that the being has become so aware that no darkness remains, all has become illuminated. A lamp of awareness has been lit deep within. Samadhi does not mean sleep and unconsciousness; it means awareness, alertness. A man in samadhi remains aware and awake all his life, every moment, every breath. All this madness and hysteria is not samadhi. But if somebody manages to collect devotees around him, why should he say that something is wrong? – "What is happening is right, it is good!" This stupidity has been going on for thousands of years, and unfortunately there is no telling for how much longer it will continue. You are helping it to continue. I don't call chanting or repetition meditation.

Meditation means two things: making the effort to meditate and creating awareness inside oneself. And in the meditation which we are going to do tonight, don't go to sleep either! Now we will do the night meditation.

You should not go to sleep. Relax the body, relax the breath, make the mind silent – but do not go to sleep. Be totally awake inside. That's why I have told you to keep listening to everything outside, because if you are listening you will remain awake. But if you are not listening there is a possibility that you will go to sleep. Sleep is a good thing, sleep is not bad – but don't think that sleep is meditation. Sleep is necessary, but sleep is not meditation – you must remember that. If sleep does not come you can induce sleep by doing some chanting, but don't make the mistake of thinking that you might experience something spiritual. And you can make that mistake, it is not difficult. Just as a person takes sleeping pills, you can chant a mantra. It does not matter, it will work just like a sleeping pill.

When Vivekananda was in America he said something about mantras and meditation, and a newspaper reported in an article that what Vivekananda was saying sounded good because a mantra sounded like a non-medicinal tranquilizer. It was a good way to induce sleep.

If you want to induce sleep that is one thing, but to bring about a state of meditation is a totally different thing.

So in the experiment that we are doing here, everyone should become relaxed, everyone should go on listening, but everyone has to remain totally alert inside. Tomorrow we will talk more about the phenomenon of staying alert, then things will be clearer to you.

Before doing this experiment, try to understand a few things. Firstly, this is a very simple experiment. Don't get the idea in your mind that you are doing something very difficult. Whatever you think of as difficult becomes difficult not because it is difficult, but because your thinking makes it so. Whatever you think of as easy becomes easy. The difficulty is in your vision.

You have been told for thousands of years that meditation is a very difficult thing, that it is available only to some rare people, that it is like walking on the edge of a sword, and this and that.... All these things have created a feeling in your mind that meditation is for rare people, that it is not for everybody. "All that we can do is pray and worship, or chant 'Ram, Ram' or sing some devotional songs non-stop for days together, usually very loudly into a microphone so that not only are we benefited, but all the neighbors also!" You think that this is all that is possible for you and meditation is only for the very few. This is all wrong.

Meditation is possible for every person. Meditation is so simple that it is difficult to find a man for whom meditation is not possible. But you have to prepare: you have to understand your capacity, your role and your attitude when you enter into such simplicity. It is very simple, it is as simple as the most simple thing can be.

As simply as a bud becomes a flower, just as simply, man's mind can become meditative. But for a bud to become a flower, light, water and fertilizer are needed. This is natural, these are its needs. In the same way, the mind has a certain need to become meditative. And this is what we are talking about.

Yesterday we talked about the needs of the body; today we have talked about how to create a healthy mind, how to become free of the entangling net of the mind. And tomorrow we will talk about the heart, the second center. If the heart and the mind are understood, then it will be very easy to enter into the third center.

There may be some new people here today, so I must tell them that we will now lie down for the meditation. This is a night meditation, to be done lying down before going to sleep. So everybody, find your own space and lie down without touching anybody else. Some people can come up here and some can lie down on the floor in front.

CHAPTER SEVEN

TUNING THE HEART

MY BELOVED ONES,

The center of thinking is the mind, the center of feeling is the heart, and the center of life-energy is the navel. Thinking and contemplation happen through the mind. We talked a little about the center of thought yesterday. Feeling, experiencing emotions such as love, hate and anger, happens through the heart. Life-energy happens through the navel.

On the first day I told you that the mind is very tense and has to be relaxed. In thinking, there is great tension and stress, the mind is under much stress. The strings of the *veena* of thought are so taut that no music arises from them. Rather, the strings break and man becomes disturbed; he has become insane. For music to be created, it has become absolutely necessary to relax the strings of the veena of thought so that they can be in tune.

The situation of the heart is exactly opposite to that of the mind. The strings of the heart are very loose: for music to be created, they need to be tightened a little so that they can also be in tune. The tension in the strings of thought has to be reduced and the loose strings of the heart have to be tightened a little.

If the strings of both thought and feeling are in tune, if they are balanced, then the music can be created through which the journey to the navel can be made.

Yesterday we talked about how thoughts can become silent; this morning we will talk about how the strings of feeling, of the heart, can be tightened.

But before you can understand this, you have to understand that mankind has been living under a curse for centuries, and the curse is that he has condemned all the qualities of the heart. He has considered all the qualities of the heart to be a curse, not a blessing. This ignorance, this mistake, has been incalculably harmful. You have condemned anger, you have condemned pride, you have condemned hatred, you have condemned attachment – you have condemned everything. And you have done all this without understanding that all these qualities are just transformations of the same qualities that you praise. You have praised compassion and you have condemned anger, without understanding that compassion is a transformed form of the energy of anger itself. You have condemned hate and you have praised love, without understanding that the energy which appears as hate can be transformed and reappear as love. The energy behind both of these is not different. You have condemned pride and you have praised humbleness, without understanding that the same energy which appears as pride becomes humbleness. There is no basic conflict between these two, they are two aspects of the same energy.

If the strings of the veena are too loose or too tight and a musician touches them, the sound that is created is unmusical, disturbing to the ears and frightening to the mind. If to protest against this disharmonious sound a person were to get angry and break the veena's strings and throw the veena away, he can, but he should not forget that by tuning it, harmonious sounds could have been created on the same instrument. The unmusical sound is not the fault of the veena: the mistake is that the veena has not been tuned. If the veena had been tuned, then from the same strings which produce disharmony, music which is a balm for the soul could also have been created.

Musical and unmusical notes both arise from the same strings – although this appears to be absolutely contradictory – and the results of both will be opposite. One of them will lead you into a state of bliss and the other one will lead you into a state of unhappiness, but the strings and the instrument are the same.

Anger arises in man's heart if his heart is not balanced. If the same heart becomes balanced, then the energy which begins as anger starts transforming into compassion. Compassion is the transformation of anger.

If a child is born without anger, then it is certain that compassion will never appear in the life of that child. If there is no possibility of hate in the heart of a child, then there will be no possibility of love either.

But until now you have lived with the illusion that feelings like these are contradictory, and if you destroy one, then the other will take over. This is absolutely wrong. There can be no teaching more dangerous than this – it is not psychological and it is very unintelligent. Compassion does not arise through the destruction of anger: it is attained through the transformation of anger. Compassion is not the destruction of anger, it is anger that has become tuned and musical.

So if you are opposed to anger and try to destroy it, then you are trying to destroy the musical instrument. And in destroying it, your development will be very weak and feeble; none of the qualities of the heart will be able to develop in you. It is the same situation as somebody piling fertilizer around his house – which will spread dirt and a bad smell everywhere – in order for flowers to blossom. But instead of the fragrance of flowers you will get the bad smell of the fertilizer and your life will become intolerable.

Flowers will certainly blossom with fertilizer, but not by just piling it around the house. The fertilizer first has to undergo a change. It must enter the plants through the roots, and then one day the foul smell of the fertilizer will turn into the fragrance of flowers. But if somebody simply piles fertilizer around his house he will go crazy with the smell, and if he throws the fertilizer away his flowers will become lifeless and pale. The transformation of the fertilizer can change a foul smell into fragrance.

This very chemistry, this very alchemy is called yoga, religiousness. The art of transforming whatever is meaningless in life into something meaningful, is religion.

But what you are doing in the name of religion is committing suicide, you are not transforming your consciousness. You are living with some basic misunderstandings, a shadow of some deep curse hangs over you. Your hearts have remained undeveloped because you have condemned the basic qualities of the heart. It will be good to understand this more deeply.

If a person is growing rightly, anger will play an important part in his life. Anger has its own color. If it is removed, then the picture of man's life will be in some sense incomplete, some color will be missing. But from childhood you start teaching children to repress certain qualities, and the result of repressing these qualities is that the child will slowly suppress whatever you call bad, he will suppress it in himself. And a suppressed heart becomes weak because its strings are not rightly tuned. And this suppression will happen in the mind because your education does not go deeper than the mind.

When you tell children that anger is bad, this teaching will not reach to the heart. The heart has no ears to listen with and no words to think with. This teaching will go into the mind, and the mind cannot change the heart. So now a problem is created: the mind center thinks that anger is wrong, but the heart center does not; it has no connection with the mind. So every day you become angry, and every day you repent and decide not to be angry again, but the next morning you wake up and again you get angry. You are surprised because you have decided so many times not to get angry, yet it still happens.

You don't know that the center which feels angry is different from the mind center. The center which decides, "I will not be angry," is absolutely different from the center which becomes angry. They are two totally different centers. So decisions and repentance do not have any effect on your anger: you go on being angry and you go on regretting it and you go on feeling upset about it. You do not understand that these two centers are so separate that the decision taken by the one does not reach the other at all...so man disintegrates within.

The heart center works in certain ways, and needs certain things to develop. If the mind interferes in that center, it will become disturbed and chaotic. Everybody's heart center has become absolutely chaotic, absolutely disturbed. Certainly, the first thing is that anger should be transformed – but it should not be destroyed.

So the first key to tighten the strings of the heart is to develop all the qualities of the heart; none should be destroyed. You may be a little puzzled: does one need to develop anger? I say to you that one certainly has to develop anger, because anger can one day be transformed and become compassion. Otherwise compassion can never arise. If you read the life story of the most compassionate people in the world, you will find that in their early days they were very angry people. Anger has its own dignity and its own pride. If you read the life story of the greatest celibates who have existed in the world, you will find that in their early days they were very sexual people.

Gandhi became a great celibate only as a result of being very sexual when he was young. When Gandhi's father was dying, the physicians told him that his father would not be able to survive the night, but even that night Gandhi could not keep away from his wife. It was the last night of his father's life, it would have been very natural to sit with his father. It was the last farewell, he would not see his father again – but in the middle of the night Gandhi went to his wife. His father died while Gandhi was in bed with his wife. It created a very strong shock in his mind: Gandhi's celibacy developed because of this shock. The shock turned all the energy of this highly sexual mind into a desire for celibacy.

How could it happen? It could happen because energy is always neutral, there is only a change of direction. The energy which was flowing towards sex started flowing in the reverse direction.

If there is much energy already, it can flow in any other direction, but if there is no energy there is nothing that can move anywhere. What will move?

All the energies should develop rightly. The ideas of moral teachings have turned man into a very miserable and impotent being. In the past, people experienced life in a deeper way than you do.

Two Rajput youths went to the court of King Akbar. They were brothers. They went to Akbar and said, "We are looking for a job."

Akbar said, "What can you do?"

They said, "We don't know how to do anything, but we are brave people. You may need us."

Akbar said, "Have you got a certificate for bravery? What proof do you have that you are brave?"

Both of them started laughing. They said, "Can there be a certificate for bravery? We *are* brave!"

Akbar replied, "You cannot get a job without a certificate."

Again they laughed. They pulled out their swords, and within a second they had thrust the swords into each other's chests. Akbar was shocked. Both the youths were lying on the ground, blood was flowing everywhere – but they were laughing! They said, "Akbar, you don't know that there can be only one certificate for bravery, and that is death. There can be no other certificate." Then they both died. Tears came into Akbar's eyes. He had not even imagined that such a thing could happen. He called one of his Rajput military commanders and said to him, "A very grave accident has happened: two Rajput youths have killed each other. I had only asked them for a certificate!"

The commander said, "You asked something wrong. This would have made any Rajput's blood boil. What can the certificate for bravery be other than death? Only a coward and a weakling could have a certificate saying that he is brave, saying that somebody thinks he is brave. How can a brave man bring a character certificate? You asked a wrong question. You don't know at all how to talk to a Rajput. What they have done is right, there was no possibility to doing anything else. It was a clear choice."

Such intense anger! Such radiance! This kind of personality has an immense grandeur. Mankind is losing these qualities. All the radiance, all the courage and strength of man is being destroyed – and you think that you are giving him a good education! But this is not the case: your children are developing in a very wrong way, nothing of a real human being is growing inside them.

A very famous lama has written in his autobiography, "When I was five years old, I was sent to a university to study. At that time I was just five years old. My father had told me in the evening that I would be sent to the university the next morning. And he said, "Neither I nor your mother will be there to say goodbye to you. Your mother will not be there because there would be tears in her eyes, and if you saw her crying, you would go on looking back at her – and there has never been a man in our family who has looked back. I also will not be there because if you look back even once after getting on the horse, then you will no longer be my son and the doors of this house will be closed to you forever. The servants will say farewell to you tomorrow morning. Remember, do not look back after getting on the horse. There has never been a person in our family who has looked back."

Such an expectation of a five-year-old child! The five-year-old was woken up at four o'clock in the morning and put on a horse. The servants bade him farewell. As he left a servant said, "My child, be careful. You can be seen until the crossroad, your father is watching from upstairs. Do not look back before the crossroad. All the children in this house have departed in this way, but no one has looked back." And the servant also told him,

"The place where you are being sent is not an ordinary university – the greatest men in the country have studied at that university. There will be a very difficult entrance examination. So whatever happens, try in every way to pass the entrance examinations because if you fail, there will be no place for you in this house."

Such harshness with a five-year-old child! He sat on the horse, and in his autobiography he wrote that as he sat on the horse, "Tears started flowing from my eyes, but how could I look back to the house, to my father? I was leaving for the unknown. I was so small, but I could not look back because nobody in my house had ever looked back. If my father were to see it, I would be banned from my house forever. So I controlled myself and looked forward, I never looked back."

Something is being created in this child. Some willpower, some life-energy is being awakened in this child to strengthen his navel center. This father is not hard, this father is very loving. And all the mothers and fathers who seem to be loving are wrong: they are weakening their children's inner centers. No strength, no determination is being created within them.

The child reached the school. He was a five-year-old child – there was no way to know what his capacities were going to be. The principal of the school said, "The entrance test here is difficult. Sit near the door with your eyes closed and do not open them until I come back – whatever happens. This is your entrance test. If you open your eyes then we will send you back, because someone who does not have even this much strength in himself to sit with his eyes closed for a while, cannot learn anything. Then the door to learning will be closed because you will not be worthy. Then go and do something else." All this to a small child of five years....

He sat near the entrance with his eyes closed. Flies started disturbing him, but he knew that he must not open his eyes because once he opened his eyes the test would be over. The other children were coming in and out of the school: somebody started pushing him, somebody started disturbing him, but he was determined not to open his eyes; otherwise the whole thing would be spoiled. And he remembered his servants telling him that if he failed the entrance test then his father's house would be closed to him forever.

One hour passed, two hours passed – he sat with closed eyes afraid that even by mistake he might open them. There were many temptations to open his eyes: the road was busy, children were running around, flies were harassing him, some children were pushing him and throwing pebbles at him. He wanted to open his eyes to see if his master had come. One hour passed, two hours passed, three hours, four hours – he sat there for six hours!

After six hours the master came and said, "My child, your entrance test is over. Come in, you will become a youth of strong will. You have the determination within you to do whatsoever you want. To sit with closed eyes for some five or six hours at this age is a great thing." The master hugged him and said, "Don't be worried, those children were told to harass you. They were told to disturb you a little so that you would be tempted to open your eyes."

The lama wrote, "At the time, I thought I was being treated very harshly, but now at the end of my life I am full of gratefulness towards those people who were hard on me. They awakened something in me, some dormant strength became active."

You are doing the opposite. You say, "Don't be angry with the children, don't beat them." Now all over the world, corporal punishment has been absolutely stopped. A child cannot be hit, no physical punishment can be given to a child. This is not wise because a punishment is out of love, it is not given with enmity. Those children who are given some kind of punishment, their centers awaken within them. The backbone is straightened and strengthened. A determination arises within them. Anger and pride also arise, and an inner strength is born and can grow.

We are creating people without spines who can only crawl on the earth and cannot fly like eagles in the sky. We are creating a creeping, crawling man who has no spine. And we think that we are doing it out of compassion and love and morality.

You teach man not to become angry, you teach him not to express any intensity, you teach him to become weak and wishy-washy. There can be no soul in the life of such a man. There can be no soul within this man because he cannot have the intense feelings of the heart within him which are necessary for the soul.

There was a Mohammedan king, Omar. He had been in great difficulty, at war with a man for twelve years. In the last battle he killed his enemy's horse, knocked the man to the ground and sat on his chest. He lifted his spear and was about to plunge it into his chest when his enemy spat in his face. Omar threw away the spear and stood up. His enemy was amazed. He said, "Omar, after twelve years you finally have the chance to kill me. Why have you missed it?"

Omar said, "I was thinking that you are an enemy worthy of me, but by spitting in my face you have shown such pettiness that now there is no question of killing you. The pettiness that you have shown is not the quality of a brave man. I had been thinking that you were my equal, so for twelve years I continued the war. But when I was going to kill you with the spear, you spat at me – this is not the behavior of a brave man. I will be committing a sin if I kill you. What will the world say to me if I were to kill someone so weak that he could only spit at me? The matter is finished. I am not going to commit a sin by killing you."

Those were wonderful people. The invention of modern weapons and armaments has destroyed all that was significant in human beings. Face-to-face battles had their own value. They used to expose whatever was hidden inside a man. Today, not a single soldier fights directly – he throws a bomb from an airplane.

This has no relation to bravery, this has no relation to the inner qualities – he simply sits and presses the button of a machine gun.

The possibility of awakening what is hidden in man's inner being has become less, and it is not surprising when man has become so weak and feeble. His authentic being cannot develop. All the elements within him cannot unite together and be expressed, manifested.

Our educational systems are surprising. According to me, all the heart qualities within man should be intensely and extremely developed; this should be the priority. Only if there is extreme development can there be transformation. All transformation takes place at extreme points, no transformation happens below that. If water is heated, it does not evaporate when it is lukewarm. Lukewarm water is also water, but at a hundred degrees, when the water reaches its ultimate temperature, then a transformation takes place and the water starts evaporating. Water turns into vapor at a hundred degrees, it does not become vapor before that. Lukewarm water does not become vapor.

You all are lukewarm people – no transformation can take place in your life. All the qualities of your mind and of your heart should be developed to the utmost; only then can there be a revolution in them. Only then can there be a change. When anger has an intensity it can be transformed into compassion, otherwise not.

But you are the enemies of anger, of greed, of passion and so you become just lukewarm people. Then life remains just lukewarm and no transformation can ever happen. This lukewarmness has had a tremendously harmful effect on human beings.

In my vision, the first thing that has to be understood is that all the qualities of your personality, of your heart, should develop rightly. Intense anger has a beauty of its own which may not be apparent to you. Intense anger has a radiance, an energy, a meaning. It contributes to the personality in its own way. All the feelings of the heart should be intensely developed.

So the first point is that the qualities of the heart should be developed, not destroyed.

What is the second point? The second point is that there should be awareness, but no suppression. The more you suppress the feelings of the heart, the more they become unconscious.

We lose sight of whatever we suppress: it moves into darkness. All the energies of the heart should be clearly looked at. If you feel angry don't try to suppress it by chanting 'Rama, Rama'. If you feel angry, sit alone in a room, close the door and meditate on the anger. See the anger totally – "What is this anger? What is the energy of this anger? From where does this anger arise? Why does it arise? How does it surround my mind and influence me?"

In aloneness, meditate on anger. See the anger totally, understand it, recognize it – from where does it arise, why does it arise? Then slowly, slowly you will become a master of the anger. And the person who becomes a master of his anger has great power, great strength. He becomes strong, he becomes a master of himself.

So it is not a question of fighting with the anger, it is a question of knowing the anger – because remember, there is no greater energy than knowing and there is no greater stupidity than to fight with one's own energies. A person who is fighting with his own energies is committing the same mistake as a man who is wrestling with his own hands. If one hand is wrestling with the other, no hand will ever be able to win because they both belong to the same person. The energy is flowing in both hands, and if there is a fight between these two hands the energy will be dissipated, there can be no question of winning. In this kind of fight you will be defeated. All your energy will be wasted.

Whose energy is in the anger? – it is your own energy. The energy is yours, but you are the one who is fighting it. If you divide yourself and fight you will go on breaking apart; you will disintegrate, you will not be a whole person. There can be no attainment in life other than defeat for the person who fights with himself. There cannot be, it is impossible. Do not fight. Know your own energies, recognize them, be acquainted with them.

So the second point is not suppression but awareness. Do not suppress. Whenever, whatever energy arises within you do not suppress it. You are a collection of unknown energies. You are the center of very unknown energies with which you have no acquaintance, of which you have no awareness.

Thousands of years ago, when lightning would strike the earth, man would become afraid. He would fold his hands and say, "Oh God! Have you become angry? What has happened?" He was afraid, and the lightning was a cause for fear. But today we know about electricity, we have mastered it, so today it is not a cause for fear; instead it has become a servant. It gives light in every house, it helps the sick to be treated and machines to keep operating. Man's whole life is influenced by it and run by it. Man has become the master of electricity. But for thousands of years he was afraid of it because he did not know what electricity was. Once we came to know what it was, then we became its master.

Knowing makes you a master. Within you, many energies greater than electricity are alight, they shine. Anger glows, hatred glows, love glows. You become afraid of what is happening because you do not know what all these energies are.

Make your life an inner laboratory and start knowing all these energies within – watch them, recognize them. Never suppress, even unintentionally. Never be afraid, even by mistake, but try to know whatever is within you. If anger comes, then feel fortunate and be thankful to the person who has made you angry: he has given you an opportunity – some energy has arisen within you and now you can look at it. Look at it silently, in aloneness; search to see what it is.

The more your knowing grows, the deeper your understanding will become. The more you become a master of your anger, the more you will find that it is under your control. The day you become a master of your anger will be the day you can transform it.

You can transform only that which you are master of; you cannot change that which you are not a master of. And remember, you can never be a master of something that you fight with because it is impossible to become the master of an enemy; one can only be the master of a friend. If you become an enemy of the energies within yourself, then you can never become master of them. You can never win without love and friendship.

Neither be afraid of nor condemn the infinite treasure of the energies within you. Start knowing what is hidden within you.

So much is hidden within man – there is no limit. We are not yet even at the beginning of humanity. Perhaps after ten or twenty-five thousand years humanity will be as far away from us as the monkeys are now. A totally new race can evolve – because as yet we have no idea of how many energies are within man.

Scientists say that about half of man's brain is still absolutely unused, no use is being made of it at all. Just a small part of the brain is being used and the remaining part is lying idle. This remaining part cannot be useless because nothing is useless in nature. It may be that if man's experience and knowledge to grow, the part which is lying idle will become active and start to function. Then it is beyond imagining what man will be able to know.

If a man is blind then there is nothing like light in his world. Light does not exist for him. If there are no eyes, there is no light. Those animals who do not have eyes do not even know that light exists in the world. They cannot even imagine, they cannot even dream that light exists. We have five senses. Who knows? – if we had a sixth sense, maybe we would know of many more things which exist in the world. And if there were seven senses, then we could know even more things. Who knows what the limits of our senses are and how great they could become?

We know very little and we live even less than that. The more we know about the inner, the more we can enter the inner, the more we become acquainted with the inner, the more our life-energies will develop and our soul will crystallize.

The second key to keep in mind is that you should not suppress any of your energies: you should know them, recognize them, look into them and see them. From this you will have a very surprising experience: if you try to look at anger, if sitting silently you look deeply into it, then the anger will disappear. As you watch the anger, it disappears. If when sexual feelings arise in your mind you go on watching them, you will find that they will disappear. You will find that this sexuality arises in unconsciousness, and it disappears by observing it.

Then you will realize that you have discovered an amazing method: you will have discovered that only in unconsciousness do anger, sex and greed have power over you. Watching them, bringing your awareness to them, they all disappear.

I had a friend who had a problem with anger. He said, "I am very disturbed by it and how much it is beyond my control. Show me a method to control it without me having to do something myself – because I have almost given up, I don't think I can do anything about it. I don't think that I can get out of this anger by my own efforts."

I gave him a paper on which were written the words: now I am getting angry. I told him, "Keep this paper in your pocket, and whenever you feel angry take it out, read it and put it back again." And I said, "You can do at least this much, this is the minimum; I can't give you less to do. Read this paper and then put it back in your pocket." He said he would try.

After two or three months, when I met him again I asked, "What happened?"

He said, "I am surprised. This paper has worked like a mantra. Whenever I feel angry I take it out. The moment I take it out, my hands and feet become numb. As I am putting my hand in my pocket, I realize that I am feeling angry and then something in me loosens up; the grip that the anger used to have on me inside suddenly disappears. As my hand goes into the pocket, it relaxes and there is no longer any need to even read it. When I feel the anger I start seeing the paper in my pocket." He asked me, "How did the paper have this effect? What is the secret?"

I said, "There is no secret to it. It is simple: whenever you are unconscious, the perversions, the imbalances and the chaos of the mind take hold of you. But when you become aware everything disappears."

So watching will have two results: first, your knowledge of your own energies will develop, and knowing them makes you the master; and second, the strength of the grip which these energies have on you will decrease. Slowly, slowly you will find that at first anger comes and *then* you watch; then after a while, gradually, you will find that when anger comes, the watchfulness will come at the same time. And finally you will find that when the anger is about to arise, the watchfulness is already there. From the day when the watchfulness comes before the anger, there will no longer be any possibility for anger to arise.

Awareness of things before they happen has a value. Being sorry has no value, because it happens afterwards, and nothing can be done afterwards. Crying and weeping later on is futile because it is impossible to undo whatever has happened. There is no chance of going back, no way, no door. But whatever has not happened yet can be changed. Being sorry is simply experiencing pain after something has happened. It is meaningless, it is absolutely unintelligent. You became angry – this was a mistake; and now you are sorry – this is one more mistake. You are becoming unnecessarily disturbed. It has no value. What is needed is an awareness beforehand. Such an awareness will develop as you slowly, slowly watch all the emotions of the heart.

The second key is watching and not suppressing.

And the third key is transformation.

Each quality of the heart can be transformed. Everything has many forms, everything can change into an opposite form. There is no quality or energy which cannot be diverted towards good, towards benediction. And remember, that which can become bad can always become good; that which can become harmful can always become helpful. Helpful and harmful, good and bad are directions. It is only a question of transforming by changing the direction and things will become different.

A man was running in the direction away from Delhi. He stopped and asked somebody, "How far is it to Delhi?"

The man replied, "If you go on running in the direction you are going, you will have to run around the world before you reach Delhi because right now you are running away from it! However, if you turn around, then Delhi is the nearest town. It is only a matter of turning around."

In the direction the man was running, it would have taken him a long time to reach Delhi, but if he made a one-hundred-and-eighty-degree turn, he would already be there.

If you go on moving in the direction you are moving now, you will reach nowhere. You cannot reach anywhere even if you go around the whole earth. Because the earth is small and the mind is huge, a man may go around the earth, but to move around the mind is impossible – it is vast, infinite. You can go all the way around the earth – the man can get back to Delhi – but the mind is far bigger than the earth, and to move around it is a very long journey. So this understanding of making a complete turnaround, a complete change of direction, is the third point to be kept in mind.

The way you are moving now is wrong. What is the proof that something is wrong? The proof that something is wrong is that the more you move, the more you become empty; the more you move, the more you become sad; the more you move, the more you become restless; the more you move, the more you are filled with darkness. If this is the situation, then certainly you are moving wrongly.

Bliss is the only criterion for life. If your life is not blissful, then know that you are moving wrongly. Suffering is the criterion of being wrong, and bliss is the criterion of being right – there are no other criteria. There is no need to read any scriptures nor is there any need to ask a guru. All that is needed is to see if you are becoming more and more blissful, if your bliss is going deeper and deeper. If it is, you are moving rightly. And if suffering, pain and anguish are growing, then you are moving wrongly. There is no question of believing somebody else; it is a question of looking into your own life every day and seeing whether you are becoming more sad or more blissful. If you ask yourself there will be no difficulty.

Old people say that their childhood was very joyful. What does this mean? Have they grown in some wrong way? Childhood, the time of joy, was the beginning of life, and now at the end of life they are sad. The beginning was joyful and the end is sad...then life has moved in some wrong way. The contrary should have happened. What should have happened is that the joy of childhood should have grown day by day as the man grew. Then, in his old age, he would say that his childhood was the most painful state because it was the beginning of life, it was the first stage.

If a student has gone to a university to study and then says that slowly, slowly the knowledge he had when he first started to study is disappearing, we would ask him, "Aren't you learning? Aren't you acquiring any knowledge? This is very strange." We could have understood if he had said that he was more ignorant at the beginning of his studies. Naturally, after studying for a few years, a student should know more, not less. But to say that he now knows less sounds very strange.

People always say that they were more joyful when they were children. Poets sing songs of a blissful childhood. They must be mad. If childhood was blissful, then does it mean that because you are sad now, you have wasted your life? It would have been better if you had died in childhood – at least you would have died blissfully. Now you will die in sorrow. So those who die in childhood are fortunate.

The longer a person lives, the more his joy should grow – but your joy decreases. The poets are not saying something wrong: they are sharing their life experiences. They are correct. Your joy goes on decreasing.

Day by day, everything goes on decreasing when in fact it should be increasing. So you are growing in a wrong way.

The direction of your life is wrong, your energy is wrong. One should be constantly vigilant, constantly inquiring; one should keep the criteria clearly in one's mind. If the criteria are clear to you, and if you see that you are moving wrongly, then nobody except yourself is preventing you from moving in the right direction.

One evening two monks arrived at their hut. For four months they had been away traveling, but now, as it was the rainy season, they had returned to their hut. But when they reached their hut, the younger monk who was walking ahead suddenly became angry and sad: the winds of the storm had carried away half of the hut and only half of it was left. They had come back after four months in the hope that they would be able to rest in the hut and be safe from the rain, but now it was going to be difficult. Half of the hut had fallen down and half of its roof had been blown away by the winds.

The young monk said to his old companion, "This is too much! These are the things which create doubt about the existence of God in me. The sinners have palaces in the cities, nothing has happened to them, but the huts of poor people like us who spend day and night in prayer, is in ruins. I doubt whether God exists! Is this prayer business for real, or are we making a mistake? Maybe it is better to sin – because the palaces of the sinful stand safe and the huts of the people who pray are blown away by the winds."

The young monk was full of anger and condemnation and he felt that all his prayers were futile. But his old companion raised his folded hands towards the sky, and tears of joy started flowing from his eyes. The young man was surprised. He said,"What are you doing?"

The old man said, "I am thanking God, because who knows what the winds might have done? They could have blown away the whole hut, but God must have created some obstacles for the wind and in that way saved half our hut for us. God is concerned about us poor people also, so we should thank him. Our prayers have been heard, our prayers have not been futile – otherwise the whole roof might have been blown away."

That night both of them slept – but as you can imagine, both slept in different ways. The one who was full of anger and rage, who thought that all his prayers were futile, kept on changing his position all night and all kinds of nightmares and worries were racing around in his mind. He was worried. There were clouds in the sky, it was about to rain. Half of the roof had been blown away by the winds and they could see the sky. Tomorrow the rain would start – then what would happen?

The other slept a very deep sleep. Who else can sleep so peacefully except someone whose being is filled with gratitude and thankfulness? He got up in the morning and started dancing and singing a song. In the song he said, "Oh God, we didn't know that there could be so much bliss in a broken-down hut. If we had known it before, then we would not have even bothered your winds, we ourselves would have taken away half of the roof. I have never slept so blissfully. Because half of the roof was not there, whenever I opened my eyes during the night I saw the stars and the gathering clouds in your sky. And now that the rains are about to start, it will be even more beautiful because with half the roof gone, we will be able to hear the music of your raindrops much more clearly. We have been idiots. We have spent so many rainy seasons sheltering inside the hut. We had no idea what joy it could be to be exposed to the sky and the wind and the rain. If we had realized it, we would not have bothered your winds; we our-selves would have got rid of half the roof."

The young man asked, "What is this I am hearing? What is all this nonsense? What is this madness? What are you saying?"

The old man said, "I have looked at things deeply, and my experience is that whatever makes us more happy is the right direction in life for us, and whatever makes us suffer more is the wrong direction. I thanked God and my bliss increased. You became angry at God and your anguish increased. You were restless last night, I slept peacefully. Now I am able to sing a song and you are burning with anger. Very early, I came to understand that the direction in which life becomes more blissful is the right direction – and I have focused my whole consciousness towards that direction. I don't know whether God exists or not. I don't know whether he has heard our prayers or not, but my proof is that I am happy and dancing and you are crying and angry and worried. My bliss proves that my way of living is right and your anguish proves that the way you are living is wrong."

The third point is to keep a continuous check on which direction it is that deepens your joy. There is no need to ask anybody else. You can use this criterion every day, in your daily life. The criterion is bliss. It is just like the criterion for testing gold by rubbing it on a stone: the goldsmith will throw away whatever is not pure and put whatever is pure into his vault. Go on checking every day using the criterion of bliss, see what is right and what is wrong. Whatever is wrong can be thrown away, and whatever is right will slowly start accumulating like a treasure.

These are the three keys for the morning. In the evening we will talk a little more about them.

Now we will sit for the morning meditation. It will be better if you sit keeping a little distance from each other. Nobody should be touching anybody else. You need to understand two things; I'll explain again because perhaps some new friends are here. What we are going to do is a very simple and easy thing – but often it happens that the easy things seem very difficult to do because you are not used to doing simple things. You are accustomed to doing difficult things, not easy things.

Firstly, it is very easy and simple to allow your body

to be absolutely relaxed and silent for awhile. Close your eyes slowly and just remain sitting, without doing anything. And then secondly, silently listen to the sounds that are happening around, just listen. Just listening will start creating a silence and a depth inside.

In Japan the word they use for meditation is very interesting. They call it *zazen*. 'Zazen' means 'just sitting, doing nothing'. It means only this and nothing else: sit silently and do nothing. It is a very meaningful word.

So sit silently, doing nothing. Eyes are closed, ears are open, so the ears will listen. Just go on silently listening...go on silently listening. While listening you will find that within you a deep silence and emptiness has arisen. It is into this emptiness that one has to go on moving deeper and deeper, deeper and deeper. It is through the door of this emptiness that some day you will realize the whole.

Through this door of emptiness you will attain to that which is whole. And in this way, becoming more and more silent, listening to the birds and the sounds around you, one day you will start to hear the sound of your inner being. So we will listen silently.

Firstly, relax the body completely. Then easily, slowly, gently, close the eyes. Drop the eyelids very slowly, so that there is no weight on the eyes. Close the eyes and relax the body. Sit absolutely silently – we are sitting silently and doing nothing. There are sounds of birds all around: just listen to them silently. Keep listening to all the sounds around you. Just keep listening and don't do anything. Slowly, slowly within you something will become silent, something will settle. Just listen...and a silence will descend inside you. For ten minutes listen silently. Listen, absolutely relaxed. Listen...mind has become silent, mind has become absolutely silent, mind has become silent, mind has become silent. In deep silence...listen to each sound. Birds are singing ...listen....

CHAPTER EIGHT

LOVE HAS NO I

My beloved ones,

Tonight is the final meeting of the meditation camp, and in this last meeting I want to talk to you about some last keys.

In the mind of man there is intense tension, and this tension has reached a level of near madness. One has to relax this tension. And along with it there is much looseness in the heart of man. The strings of the *veena* of his heart are loose – they have to be tightened. This morning I told you of a few keys about tightening the strings of the heart. And now we will talk about the last key.

From the veena of man's life, the greatest music possible arises in the heart whose strings are in tune. A society which has lost its heart, an age or period in which all the values of the heart have become weakened, has lost all that is good, truthful and beautiful. If we want goodness, truth and beauty to enter our lives, there is no other way than to tune the strings of the veena of the heart.

Love is the way to tune the strings of the heart, the way to bring the strings of the heart into the right space from where music can arise. That is why I call love 'prayer'; I call love the way to attaining to the divine; I call love, 'the divine'. Prayer without love is false, hollow, meaningless. Without love, words of prayer have no value at all. And without love, no one who becomes interested in the journey towards the divine will ever be able to reach the ultimate. Love is the way to make the veena of the heart sing. You will need to understand some things about love itself.

The first illusion is that you all think you know about love. This illusion is tremendously harmful because you will never make any effort to attain to or to awaken that which you think you already know.

But you are not aware that one who knows love has simultaneously acquired the capacity to know the divine. If you know love, then nothing else remains to be known in life. But the way you are, you know nothing; everything is still to be known.

So the love which you think of as love is probably not love. You have called something else love, and as long as you have this illusion, as long as you have the idea that you know all about love, how can you search and seek for it? The first thing to be understood is that you don't know love at all.

One hot afternoon, Jesus stopped under a tree in a garden. It was very hot and he was tired, so he slept in the shadow of a tree. He did not even know to whom the house, the garden or the tree belonged. It was the garden of Magdalene, a very beautiful prostitute of those days.

Magdalene looked out the window and saw this beautiful person sleeping under the tree. She had never seen such a beautiful man. Just as there is a beauty of the body, there is a beauty of the soul. One can often see beauty of the body, but beauty of the soul is rarely seen. But when the beauty of the soul appears, even the ugliest body becomes the most beautiful flower. She had seen many beautiful people because there was always a crowd at her door – it was often difficult for her even to enter her own house. Magdalene was drawn to the tree as if pulled by some magnet.

Jesus was about to get up and leave; he had finished resting. Magdalene said, "Would you do me the favor of coming into my house to rest?"

Jesus said, "I have finished resting now, and it was your tree. Now it is time for me to leave. But if I happen to pass by here again and I am tired, then I will certainly rest in your house."

Magdalene felt hurt. Great princes had been turned away from her door, and now when she was inviting a beggar from the streets to rest in her house, he refused. It hurt her feelings, so she said, "No, I am not going to listen to this. You must come inside – won't you do even this much to show me your love? Won't you come and rest in my house for a little while?"

Jesus said, "By your very invitation I have entered your house already, because except in the feelings of the heart, where else is your house? And if you ask, 'Won't you show me even this much love?' then I will say to you that you may have seen many people who have said to you 'I love you', but none of them loved you, because in their innermost core they were loving something else. And I can assure you that I am actually one of the few people who can love you and who does love you – because only one in whose heart love has arisen can love."

None of you can love because within you there is no flow of love. When you say to somebody, "I love you," you are in fact not giving love, you are asking for love. All of you ask for love, and how can one who is himself asking for love, give love? How can beggars be emperors? How can people who are asking for love be the givers of love?

All of you ask each other for love. Your beings are beggars asking someone to love you. The wife asks the husband for love, the husband asks the wife for love; the mother asks the son, the son asks the mother; friends ask friends for love. All of you ask one another for love without realizing that the friend that you are asking is himself asking for love. You are like two beggars standing in front of each other holding your begging bowls.

As long as someone is asking for love, he cannot be capable of giving love because the very asking is an indication that there is no source of love within him. Otherwise, why would he have to ask for love from the outside? Only a person who has risen above the need to ask for love can give love. Love is a sharing, it is not a begging. Love is an emperor, it is not a beggar. Love knows only giving, it does not know anything about asking.

Do you know love? The love which is asked for cannot be love. And remember, someone who asks for love will never get any love in this world. One of the essential laws, one of the eternal laws of life is: someone who asks for love will never, ever get it.

Love only comes to the door of a house from where the desire for love has disappeared. Love starts showering on the house of someone who has stopped asking for love.

But no rains will fall on the house of someone who is still hankering for love; love will not flow towards an asking heart. The asking heart does not have the kind of receptivity that makes it possible for love to enter. Only a sharing heart, a giving heart has the kind of receptivity for love to come to its door and say, "Open the door, I have come!"

Has love ever knocked at your doors? No, because until now, you have not been able to give love. And remember also that whatsoever you give will come back to you. One of the eternal laws of life is that whatever we give comes back to us.

The whole world is nothing more than an echo: you give hate and hate will come back to you; you give anger and anger will come back to you; you abuse others and abuses return to you; you put out thorns and thorns will return to you. Whatever you have given returns to you, comes back to you in infinite ways. And if you share love, then love will come back to you in infinite ways. If love has not returned to you in an immeasurable number of ways, then know that it is because you have not given love.

But how can you give love? You don't have it to give. If you have love, then why do you wander from door to door asking for it? Why do you become beggars, wandering from place to place? Why do you ask for love?

There was a *fakir* named Farid. The people of his town said to him, "Farid, the emperor Akbar respects you very much – ask him to open a school in our town."

Farid said, "I have never asked for anything from anybody. I am a fakir, I know only giving."

The people of the town were very surprised. They said, "We have always thought that a fakir always asks, but you say that a fakir only knows how to give. We do not understand these subtle and serious things. Please just do us a favor: ask Akbar to open a school for us."

The people of the town were persistent, so early in the morning Farid went to meet Akbar. Akbar was praying in his mosque and Farid went and stood behind him. After Akbar had finished his prayers he raised both his hands towards the sky and cried, "Oh, God! Increase my wealth, increase my treasure, increase my kingdom."

Hearing this, Farid started to turn away. Akbar got up and saw that Farid was leaving. He rushed after him and stopped him, asking, "Why did you come and why are you leaving?"

Farid said, "I thought that you were an emperor, but I have found that you also are a beggar. I thought that I would ask for a school for the town – I did not know that you also ask God to increase your wealth and your treasure. It does not seem right to ask for something from a beggar. I thought that you were an emperor and now I see that you are a beggar, so I am leaving."

You are all beggars, and you all go on asking other

beggars for that which they don't have. And when you don't get it, you become sad: you weep and cry and feel that you are not getting love.

Love is not something to be obtained from the outside: love is the music of your inner being. Nobody can give you love. Love can arise within you but it cannot be obtained from the outside. There is no shop, no market, no salesman from whom you can purchase love. Love cannot be purchased at any price.

Love is an inner flowering; it arises from some dormant energy within. Yet all of us search for love on the outside. All of us search for love in the beloved – which is an absolutely wrong and futile thing to do.

Search for love within yourself. You cannot even imagine that there might be love inside yourself because love is always associated with the idea of a beloved. It gives you the idea of someone else outside. And because you don't remember how love can arise within you, the energy of love remains dormant. You don't realize that you are always asking for something outside which is already within you. And because you are asking for it outside, you do not look inside. Then that which could have arisen within, never does.

Love is the essential treasure with which each individual is born. Man is not born with money, money is social accumulation. But man is born with love. It is his birthright, it is his individual wealth, it is within him. It is a companion which was given to him at birth and which has accompanied him his whole life. But very few are fortunate enough to look within and to see where love is, how it can be found and how it can be developed. So you are born, but your wealth remains unexplored. In fact it is never explored at all, and you go on begging at others' doors, holding out your hands because you want love.

All over the world there is only one desire: for love. And all over the world there is only one complaint: I am not getting any love. And when you do not get love, you accuse others of being at fault because you do not get love. The wife says to her husband, "There is something wrong with you, that's why I am not getting any love." The husband says to his wife, "There is something wrong with you, that's why I'm not getting any love." And no one ever wonders if it has ever been possible to get love from the outside.

Love is the inner treasure – and love itself is the music of the veena of the heart.

The veena of man's heart has become very disturbed: the music for which it was created does not arise. How can this music be created? What is the obstacle standing in the way of the creation of this music? What is the obstacle which does not allow it to happen? Have you ever thought about this obstacle? Have you ever considered what it might be?

An actor who was a good dramatist and a good poet died. Many people gathered at the cremation ground for his funeral. The director of the film company in which he had been working was also present, and he said a few words of condolence.

The director said, "I made this man an actor. It was I who took him out of the back roads and put him on the highways. It was I who gave him his first role in the movies. It was I who published his first book. I am the reason he became famous all over the world!"

He had said this much...I was present at that funeral, and some of you may also have been there...the director had said this much when suddenly the corpse which was lying there got up and said, "Excuse me, sir, who is being buried here, you or me? Who are you talking about?"

The director was saying, "*I* am the one who made him famous, *I* am the one who published his book, *I* am the one who gave him his first role in the movies.... *I* am the one."

Even the corpse could not tolerate the noise of this I. It got up and said, "Forgive me, but please tell me one thing: who is being buried in this funeral, you or me? Who are you talking about?" Even corpses cannot tolerate the noise of this I – and man continuously goes on making the noise of this I. How can living people tolerate it?

There can be only two possible voices within you – but there is no voice of love within the person who is filled with the voice of I; and there is no voice of I within the person who is filled with the voice of love. The two of them can never be found together, it is impossible. It is as impossible as darkness and light existing together.

Once darkness went to God and said, "The sun keeps chasing after me. He is giving me so much trouble – he follows me from morning until night, and by the evening I am very tired. And when it is night, before I have completed my sleep and my rest, he starts to follow me again. I don't remember doing anything wrong to him, I don't think that I have ever made him angry. So why is he following me? Why am I continuously being harassed? What have I done wrong?"

Then God called the sun and asked, "Why are you chasing after that poor darkness? She is always moving, hiding, taking shelter here and there. Why do you follow her all the time? What is the need?"

The sun said, "Who is this darkness? I have not yet met her. I don't even know her. Who is darkness? What is darkness? I have not seen her yet, I have not met her yet. But if I have unknowingly committed some mistake, then I am ready to apologize. And once I recognize her, I will never follow her again."

They say that millions and trillions of years have passed since this event, but the case is still pending in the files of God. Yet God has not been able to get darkness and the sun together. And I say to you that never in the future will he be able to do so, howsoever almighty he may be. Even the almighty does not have the ability to bring darkness in front of the sun, because darkness and light cannot exist together.

There is a reason why they cannot exist together. The reason is that darkness has no being of its own, so it cannot exist in front of the sun. Darkness is only the absence of light – so how can the absence and the presence of the same thing exist together? Darkness is only the absence of the sun. Darkness is nothing in itself, it is just the absence of the sun – it is just the absence of light. So how can an absence of light exist? How can both of these things exist together? God will never be able to arrange it.

In the same way, ego and love also cannot exist together. Ego is like darkness: it is the absence of love, it is not the presence of love. Love is absent within you, so within you the voice of your I goes on echoing. And with this voice of your I you say, "I want to love, I want to give love, I want to receive love." Have you gone mad? There has never been any relationship between I and love. And this I goes on speaking about love, saying, "I want to pray, I want to attain to God, I want to be liberated."

This is the same as darkness saying, "I want to hug the sun, I want to love the sun, I want to be a guest in the house of the sun." It is impossible.

I is the absence of love itself – I is the lack of love. And the more you go on strengthening this voice of your I, the less possible it will be to find love within you. The more the ego is there, the more love will be absent. And when there is total ego, love totally dies.

There can be no love within you because if you look inside, you will find that the voice of your I is resounding there continuously, twenty-four hours a day. You breathe with this I, you drink water with this I, you enter a temple with this I. What else is there in your life except this I ?

Your clothes are the clothes of your I, your positions are the positions of your I, your knowledge is the knowledge of your I, your spiritual practice, your helping others, is the helping of your I, your everything – even your meditation – is also the meditation of your I. A strong feeling arises inside: "I am a meditator. I am not a householder, I am not an ordinary person – I am a meditator. I am a helper; I am a knowledgeable person, I am rich" – I am this, I am that....

The house that has been built around this I will never know love. And then the music which could bring the heart to the innermost core, which could make it acquainted with the truths of life, will not arise from the veena of the heart. That door will not open, it will always remain closed.

It has to be completely understood how strong your I is, how deep it is. And you have to clearly see if you are giving it more strength, if you are making it deeper, if you are making it stronger and stronger every day. And if you are making it stronger yourself, then drop any hope that love will arise within you, or that the closed knot of love can open, or that the treasure of love can be attained. Drop the very idea – there is no way that it can happen.

So I do not tell you to start loving, because the ego can also say, "I am a lover and I love."

The love which comes from the ego is absolutely false. Hence I say that all your love is false – because it comes out of ego, it is the shadow of ego. And remember, that love which comes out of ego is more dangerous than hate because hate is clear, direct and simple, but love which comes with a false face will be difficult to recognize.

If you are loved by a love that comes out of ego, after a while you will feel that you are being held by iron chains instead of loving hands. After a while you will come to know that the love which makes beautiful speeches and sings beautiful songs to you is just making tempting overtures – there is much poison in those sweet songs. And if a love which comes in the form of flowers is a shadow of the ego, then when you touch the flowers you will find thorns which will pierce you.

When people go fishing they put bait on the hook. The ego wants to become a master of others, it wants to possess them, so it pierces them deeply by baiting the hook with love. So many people end up in pain and suffering because of their illusions about love. Not even in hell do so many people suffer so much. And because of this illusion of love, the whole earth, the whole of humanity is suffering. But still you do not understand that a love from the ego is false. This is why this hell has been created.

The love to which ego is attached is a form of jealousy – and this is why no one is as jealous as lovers are. The love which is attached to the ego is a conspiracy and a trick to possess the other. It is a conspiracy: that is why no one is as suffocating as someone who says he loves you. This situation is created because of the so-called love which comes from the ego. And there can never be any relationship between love and the ego.

Jalaluddin Rumi used to sing a song, a very beautiful song – he would go from town to town singing the song. Whenever people would ask him to tell them something about God, he would sing the song. The song was very wonderful.

In that song he said that a lover went to the door of his beloved and knocked at the door, and the beloved asked, "Who are you?"

The lover said – as all lovers say – "I am your lover." There was a silence inside. No answer came, no voice was heard from inside.

The lover started knocking loudly on the door again, but it seemed that there was no one inside. He started shouting, "Why is there silence inside? Answer me! I am your lover. I have come." But the louder he said, "I have come, I am your lover," the more silent the house became, like a graveyard. There was no answer from within.

Then he started beating his head on the door and said, "Answer at least once!"

And an answer came from inside: "There can be no space in this house for two. You say 'I have come, I am your lover – but I am already present here. There is no space for two here. The door of love can open only for those who have dropped the I. Go now! Come again another time."

The lover left. He prayed and meditated for years. Many moons passed, many sunrises and sunsets passed, many years passed, and then he returned to the door. When he knocked he again heard the same question, "Who are you?" This time the lover said, "There is no I! There is only you."

Jalaluddin Rumi said that, at this moment, the door opened.

I would not have opened the door! Jalaluddin died many years ago, so there is no way for me to tell him that the time was not right for the doors to be opened. He allowed the doors to be opened too soon – because one who says, "There is only you," still experiences himself as an I. Only someone who does not experience a 'you' does not experience himself as an I either.

So although it is wrong to say that love does not contain two, it is equally wrong to say that love contains only one. In love, neither two nor one exist. If there is a sense of the one, know well that the other is also present – because only the other can be aware of the one. Where 'you' is present, I is also present.

So I would have sent that lover away again. He said, "There is no I, there is only you" – but someone who says this is *there*, totally *there*. He has just learned a trick. The first time he had answered, "I am," and the doors remained closed; then after years of contemplation he decided to say, "I am not, only you are." But who was saying this? And why was he saying this? Someone who knows 'you' also knows I.

Remember that 'you' is the shadow of I. For someone whose I has disappeared, the you also does not remain.

So I would have sent the lover away because the beloved had said, "There is no space for two." The man did not get it; he started shouting and saying, "Where are these two? Now I'm not, there is only you."

But the beloved should have told him to leave because he had only learned a trick: he still saw two people. The beloved said that if there were no longer two, the lover would not even have tried to get him to open the door – because who is asking for the door to be opened? And who does he think will open it? In a house of two, there cannot be love.

My version is that the lover went away. Years passed, and he did not return. He never returned. Then the beloved went in search of him.

So I say that the day the shadow of your I disappears, the day neither I nor you remains, on that day you will no longer have to search for the divine – the divine will come searching for you.

No man can seek the divine because he does not have the capacity for such a search. But when somebody has become ready to disappear, has become ready to be a nobody, has become ready to become an emptiness, then the divine will certainly find him. Only the divine can seek for man, man can never seek the divine because even in seeking, the ego is present: "I am seeking, I have to attain God; I have acquired wealth; I have attained a position in parliament; I have got a big house" – now the last goal remains – "I also want to attain the divine. How can I pass up the prestige of attaining God? That will be my final victory. I must attain this victory. I must also attain to the divine." This is a proclamation, an insistence, and a search by the very ego itself.

So a religious person is not one who sets out in search of the divine: a religious person is one who sets out in search of his I – and the more he goes on searching, the more he will find that his I is not at all there. And the day the I no longer remains, on that day the door which is hiding love will open for him.

So the last thing is: search for your self, not for the divine.

You do not know anything at all about the ultimate being. Do not go in search for the divine because you do not have even the slightest idea about the divine. How will you seek that about which you have no idea at all? Where will you seek someone for whom you have no address? Where will you seek someone about whom you have no information? Where will you seek someone who has no beginning and no end, someone whose location you have no idea of? You will go mad! You will not know where to look.

But you do know one thing: you know this I of yours. So first of all you have to seek this I – find out what it is, where it is and who it is. And as you search for it you will be surprised to find that this I does not exist, it was an absolutely false notion. It was your imagination that an I exists, it was an illusion that you were nourishing.

When children are born you give them a name for the

sake of convenience. You call someone Ram, someone Krishna, someone something else. Nobody has a
name, all names are for the sake of convenience. But
later on, hearing and hearing it continuously, the person gets an illusion that this is his name: I am Ram, I
am Krishna. And if you say something bad about Ram
he will be ready to fight you: you have abused him.
And where did he get his name?

Nobody is born with a name, everyone is born nameless. But the name has a social utility. To make a label
without a name is difficult, hence we give a name. We
give you a name so that others can identify you – it has
a social utility. And if you use your own name to refer
to yourself, then there will be confusion – are you refer-
ring to yourself or to someone else? So to avoid confusion you call yourself I; 'you' is the title by which you
call another. Both titles are imaginary, social utilities.
And you construct your life around these two titles
which are simply two blank words and nothing else.
Behind them there is no truth, behind them there is no
substance. They are only names, only labels.

Once, this mistake happened. There was a little girl
called Alice. And Alice went wandering in a strange
land, a wonderland. When she reached the Queen of
Wonderland, the Queen asked Alice a question. She
said, "Did you meet somebody on the way here?" And
Alice replied, "I met nobody."

But the Queen thought that she had met someone
called Nobody. And this illusion became stronger

because then the Queen's messenger arrived, and the Queen asked him also if he had met anybody. He also said, "Nobody."

The Queen said, "This is very strange." She thought that a person called Nobody had met both Alice and the messenger. So she said to the messenger, "It seems that Nobody walks slower than you."

That statement has two meanings: one meaning is that nobody walks slower than the messenger.

The messenger became afraid because a messenger should be able to walk very fast. So he said, "No, nobody walks faster than me!"

The Queen said, "This is a difficult situation. You say that Nobody walks faster than you. But if Nobody walks faster than you, then he should have arrived before you, he should have arrived already."

By now the poor messenger realized that some kind of misunderstanding had happened and so he said, "Nobody is nobody!"

But the Queen replied, "I know that Nobody is Nobody. But who is he? Tell me. He should have arrived by now. Where is he?"

With man, the same misunderstanding happens through language Everyone's name is Nobody, no name has any more meaning than this. The whole idea of I is of nobody, not more than that. But through the misunderstanding of language the illusion is created that "I am somebody, I have a name."

Man dies and leaves his name written on stones,

hoping that perhaps the stones will last forever. We don't know if they will. All the sand on the seashores was once stone. All stones sooner or later become sand. Whether you write your name on sand or you write it on stone, it is all the same. In this long history of the world, there is no difference between sand and stone. Children write their names on the sand at the seashore – maybe they think that tomorrow people will pass by and see. But the waves come and wipe the sand clean. The older people laugh and say, "Are you mad! There is no point in writing names on sand."

But the older people write on stones, and they are unaware that sand is created out of stones. There is no difference between old people and children. In foolishness, they are all of equal age.

An emperor became a *chakravartin*. This rarely happens. A chakravartin means a master of the whole earth. An old story says that chakravartins had a special privilege which was not available to anybody else, which others could not have. They had a chance to sign their name on Mt. Sumeru, the mountain in heaven. Even in infinite time it is rare for someone to become a chakravartin, so signatures on Mt. Sumeru, the eternal mountain, are a rare phenomenon.

When the emperor became a chakravartin, he was very happy: now he had the privilege of signing his name on Mt. Sumeru. He reached the entrance of heaven with great pomp and show, accompanied by a huge army. And the doorkeeper said, "You have arrived? You can come in, but this crowd cannot come inside, they will have to go home. Have you brought some tools to carve your name with?"

The emperor replied, "I have brought the instruments."

The doorkeeper told him, "This Mt. Sumeru is infinite, but there have been so many chakravartins that now there is no space left on it to sign. So first of all you will have to erase someone's name, and then you can sign your name there because no space is left, the whole mountain is covered."

The emperor went through the gate. The mountain was infinite. Many Himalayas could have been contained in its smaller ranges, yet on its surface not even an inch of space was left. He had thought that someone became a chakravartin only after long intervals, but he had no idea that so much time had passed that even if one person became a chakravartin after a long, long time, the whole mountain would still be full, no space would be left.

The emperor became very sad and upset. The doorkeeper said to him, "Don't be sad. My father and his father, my grandfather, also used to do this job. For generations we have known that whenever you want to sign you have first to erase the surface, you can never find an empty space."

Then the emperor turned around and said, "If one can sign only after erasing somebody else's name, then it is madness – because I will sign and go, and then somebody else will come tomorrow, erase my signature and sign theirs. When this mountain is so big and there are so many names, who reads them? And what is the point? Forgive me, I am making a mistake. This is meaningless."

There are very few people of such intelligence: others have their names written on stones, on temples. They build memorials and have their names written on them and they forget that they were born without names, they have no names of their own. So on the one hand stone is wasted, and on the other hand labor is wasted. And when they die and say goodbye, they go nameless.

You do not have a name of your own. The name is the illusion visible to the outside world and the I is the illusion visible to the inside. The I and the name are two sides of the same coin. The name is visible from the outside and the I is visible from the inside. And as long as this illusion of the name and the I remains, the space from where love arises cannot open.

So the last thing that I want to say is, search a little. Go to Mt. Sumeru and see how many signatures have been put there. Do you also want to add your name by erasing the surface? Go a little closer to the mountains and watch them turning into sand. Watch the children writing their names on the sea beach. Look all around you at what we are doing. Are we wasting our lives writing names on the sand? And if you feel like this, then search a little deeper – enter into this I and seek. One day you will find that *I* is nobody; there is nobody there. There is a deep silence and peace there, but there is no

I. And the day you come to know that there is no I inside you, you have come to know the whole, that which really is – the being, the existence, the divine.

That is why I say that love is the door to the divine, and ego is the door to ignorance. Love is the door to light, and ego is the door to darkness.

I had to say this last thing before we leave. Explore love from this dimension. This exploration will begin with the ego and it will end with the attainment of love. So explore in this direction: does this shadow of the ego really exist, does this I really exist? The man who sets out on this exploration not only will not find an I but he also will attain to the divine. Someone who is tied to the stake of the I is not able to undertake the journey into the ocean of the divine. This was the last thing I wanted to say to you. In fact, this is the first and last thing to be said.

I is the first thing in a person's life and I is the last. The person tied up in the I experiences pain, and after becoming free of I he attains to bliss. There is no story, no tale except I. There is no dream except I. There is no lie except I.

Find this I, and the doors to bliss can open. If the rock of the I is shattered, the springs of love will start flowing. Then the heart will fill with the music of love. When the heart is filled with love a new journey starts which is difficult to describe in words. That journey will take you to the very center of life.

I wanted to say these few things before leaving.

Now we will sit for the night meditation. For ten

minutes we will sit for the night meditation, and then we will say goodbye. And I say goodbye to you with a hope and a prayer to God that everybody will be blessed enough to attain to love, that everybody will be blessed enough to get rid of the disease of I, that everybody will be blessed enough to find that which is already within him.

A beggar had died in a very big town...pray that you will not die like that beggar. The beggar had died after begging in the same place for forty years. He had thought that he would become an emperor through begging – but can anybody become an emperor by begging? The more a person begs, the more of a beggar he becomes.

The day he started he was a small beggar, the day he died he was a great beggar, but he did not become an emperor. He died. So the people in the neighborhood behaved in the same way with him as they did with other dead people: they took away his corpse and burned it along with the rags that he had left lying there. Then the people of the neighborhood thought that for forty years this beggar had made this very earth dirty, and it would be good to dig up some of that earth and throw it away. So they started digging.

And they had a big surprise! If the beggar had been alive he would have gone mad. After digging up the earth, they found a huge treasure buried right under the spot where the beggar used to sit and beg.

He did not know that if he had dug up the earth

underneath him, he would have become an emperor and there would have been no need to beg. But what did the poor man know? His eyes were looking outside, his hands were spread out, so he died begging. All the people of the neighborhood stood there quite shocked: "What kind of beggar was this. This idiot had not even realized that a treasure had been buried exactly in the place where he was sitting."

I went to that place and met the people of the neighborhood and I said to them, "You fools, don't be concerned about the beggar. Drop your judgments of the beggar. At some time you should also dig up the earth beneath you – because it may be that when you die, other people will laugh at you."

When a person dies, other people laugh at him saying that he was naive, he could not achieve anything in his life. And they do not know that others are just waiting for them to die so that they can also laugh and say that this person was really naive and could not achieve anything.

Living people laugh at somebody when he dies, but if a living person could get the idea of laughing at himself while he is still alive, then his life would be transformed. He would become a different person. If in these three days of the camp you have remembered to laugh at yourself, then the matter is finished. If you can remember to dig up the place where you are standing right now, then the matter is finished. Then all that I have said can certainly come to a fruition in you.

In the end, I just pray that you will not die a beggar, but an emperor. I pray that you will not give the people of the neighborhood a chance to laugh. For these days you have listened to my talks so silently and so lovingly, I am very grateful, and I bow down to the divine that is present in everybody. Please accept my greetings.

Now we will sit for the night meditation. All of you make some space so that you can lie down. This is the last meditation, so use it as totally as you can. Everybody should be at some distance from each other.

Don't talk. Nobody should talk. Those people sitting there should spread out. Nobody should be touching anybody else. Move away from there, move to where there is space. Don't talk at all because this has nothing to do with talking. Some people should come up here in the front, and be careful that nobody is disturbed because of somebody else.

First of all lie down with your body totally relaxed. Allow it to be completely loose and relaxed. Then slowly close your eyes. Close your eyes.

You have closed your eyes and have completely relaxed the body. Now I will give suggestions – go on listening, your body and mind will follow them.

Feel that the body is becoming relaxed, the body is becoming relaxed, the body is becoming relaxed, the body is becoming relaxed. Feel that the body is becoming relaxed, allow the body to be totally relaxed.... And feel in the mind that the body has become totally relaxed, the body has become relaxed, the body has become totally relaxed....

The breath is becoming silent. Feel in the mind that the breath is becoming silent, the breath is becoming silent.... The breath has become silent, the breath has become silent....

The mind is also becoming empty. The mind is becoming silent. Feel that the mind is becoming silent, the mind has become silent....

Now for ten minutes remain awake inside and keep listening silently to all the sounds around. Stay awake inside, don't go to sleep. Remain conscious inside. Stay awake inside and keep silently listening. Just keep listening. Keep listening to the silence of the night and while listening, a deep emptiness will arise....

Listen. For ten minutes keep listening silently, just listening silently. The mind is becoming completely empty. The mind is becoming empty. The mind has become empty, the mind has become empty....

The mind has become totally empty. The mind is becoming empty. Drown in the emptiness that is all around. The mind is becoming empty. The mind is becoming empty, the mind is becoming empty....

The mind is becoming silent. The mind is becoming empty. Drown more deeply. The mind is becoming empty, the mind has become completely empty....

O S H O   I S   A   M O D E R N - D A Y   Buddha whose wisdom, clarity and humor have touched the lives of millions of people around the world. He is creating the conditions for the emergence of what he calls the "New Man" – a completely new kind of human being who is aware, life-affirmative and free.

According to Osho, the spiritual traditions of the past have made a deep split within the individual, reflected in all the institutions of society. His way is to heal this split, to restore the unity of body and spirit, earth and sky.

After his enlightenment in 1953, the evolution of this New Man became his dream. In 1966, Osho left the academic world and his post as a philosophy professor at the University of Jabalpur and began touring India intensively and speaking to many hundreds of thousands of people. At the same time, Osho was developing practical tools for man's self-transformation.

By the late 1960s, Osho had begun to create his unique dynamic meditation techniques. He says that modern man is so burdened with the traditions from the past and the anxieties of modern-day living, that he must go through a deep cleansing process before he can begin to discover the thought-free, relaxed state of meditation.

By 1974, a commune had been established around Osho in Pune, India, and the trickle of visitors from the West had become a flood. Today, his Commune is the largest spiritual growth center in the world. Each year it attracts thousands of international visitors to its meditation, therapy, bodywork and creative programs.

Osho speaks on virtually every aspect of the development of human consciousness. His talks cover a staggering range – from the meaning of life and death, to the struggles of power and politics, from the challenges of love and creativity, to the significance of science and education. These talks, given over thirty years, have been recorded on audio cassette and videotape, and published in hundreds of books in every major language of the world. He belongs to no tradition and says, "My message is not a doctrine, not a philosophy. My message is a certain alchemy, a science of transformation."

Osho left his body in 1990 as a result of poisoning by US government agents, while being held in custody for technical immigration violations in 1985. He asks always to be referred to in the present tense. The words on his Samadhi, which Osho himself dictated, read:

OSHO

Never Born Never Died
Only Visited this Planet Earth between
December 11 1931 – January 19 1990

THE OSHO COMMUNE International in Pune, India, is a place to relax from the outward stresses of life and nourish the soul. Osho describes the Commune as a laboratory, an experiment in creating a "New Man" – a human being who lives in harmony with the inner and the outer, with himself and his environment, and who is free from all ideologies and conditionings that now divide humanity.

Set in 31 acres in the tree-lined suburb of Koregaon Park, this meditation resort receives thousands of visitors every year from all countries and from all walks of life. Visitors generally spend from three weeks to three months at the Commune and stay in nearby hotels and apartments.

Osho Commune houses the unique Osho Multiversity, which offers hundreds of personal growth and self-discovery programs and professional trainings throughout the year, all of which are designed to help people find the knack of meditation: the passive witnessing of thoughts, emotions and actions, without judgment or identification.

Unlike many traditional Eastern disciplines, meditation at Osho Commune is an inseparable part of daily life, whether working, relating, or just being, resulting in people not renouncing the world but bringing to it a spirit of awareness, celebration and a deep reverence for life.

Gautama the Buddha Auditorium is situated at the center of the Commune and here, six different one-hour-long meditations are offered every day.

Osho Dynamic Meditation*: Osho's technique designed to release tensions and repressed emotions, opening the way to a new vitality and an experience of profound silence.

Osho Kundalini Meditation*: Shaking free dormant energies, and through spontaneous dance and silent sitting, allowing these energies to be redirected inward.

Osho Nataraj Meditation*: The inner alchemy of dancing so totally, that the dancer disappears and only the dance remains.

Osho Nadabrahma Meditation*: Based on an ancient Tibetan humming technique to harmonize the energy flow.

Osho No-Dimensions: This is a powerful method for centering the energy, based on a Gurdjieff technique.

Osho Vipassana Meditation: Gautama the Buddha's technique of dissolving mental chatter through the awareness of breath.

The highlight of the day at the Commune is the evening meeting of the Osho White Robe Brotherhood. This two-hour celebration of music, dance and silence, followed by a videotape discourse from Osho, is unique – a deep and complete meditation where thousands of seekers, in Osho's words, "...dissolve into a sea of consciousness."

*Service mark Osho International Foundation

Suggested Further Reading

A Cup of Tea

This unique book is a compilation of intimate letters written by Osho to His disciples and friends on subjects as diverse as solitude, love, meditation and receptivity, as well as our fruitless efforts to make our lives secure, the stupidity of the human mind, and the ability to laugh at oneself.   ISBN 81 7261 013 0

Seeds of Wisdom

Seeds of Wisdom is a collection of 120 letters written by Osho to a beloved disciple.

The selections in this book are actually more like small stories and parables than letters. Using incidents in his daily life as a starting point, or recalling ancient teaching stories, Osho reflects on the nature of truth and the spiritual search, while at the same time giving the reader an intimate glimpse into his own life and search.   ISBN 81 7261 018 1

Behind a Thousand Names
Talks on the Nirvana Upanishad

First time in English. In these talks Osho explores the essential nature of spiritual longing, the moving force behind every seeker's quest for truth. "The sutra that we are exploring is so revolutionary that perhaps this is why no commentaries have ever been written on the Nirvana Upanishad. It is one of the neglected ones..."   ISBN 81 7261 015 7

VEDANTA: SEVEN STEPS TO SAMADHI
DISCOURSES ON THE AKSHYA UPANISHAD

These discourses were delivered mornings and evenings at an early meditation camp, with the day spent experiencing the meditations Osho describes. An incomparable opportunity to explore Osho's most powerful techniques.   ISBN 3 89338 120 1

AND THE FLOWERS SHOWERED
TALKS ON ZEN

Commenting on eleven Zen anecdotes, Osho explores the spiritual search – speaking on emptiness and no-mind, knowledge and being; on belief and trust, repression and truth; on philosophy and religion, love and divinity; on death and disease, on happiness and living in the here-and-now.   ISBN 81 7261 002 5

THE EMPTY BOAT
TALKS ON THE STORIES OF CHUANG TZU

Osho revitalizes the 3000-year-old Taoist message of self-realization through the stories of the Chinese mystic, Chuang Tzu. He speaks about the state of egolessness, 'the empty boat'; about spontaneity, dreams and wholeness; about living life choicelessly and meeting death with the same equanimity.
ISBN 3 89338 118 X

JUST LIKE THAT

With humor and sensitivity Osho illuminates traditional Sufi stories, revealing the hidden dimensions of Sufism, "the unteachable teaching." He distinguishes between need and desire, between

expertise and existential experience, and talks on the nature of the ego, the importance of trust and the stages of growth in one's evolution.
ISBN 3 89338 113 9

Nowhere to Go but In
Osho talks on the nature of enlightenment, the seeking of spiritual powers, the relationship between meditation and love, meditation and sex, making love with existence without a partner, and tantra.
ISBN 81 7261 017 3

The Goose is Out
Questions from seekers and friends, all attempting in so many ways – just as in the famous Zen koan – to free their goose from their bottle without either killing the goose or breaking the bottle. The goose is the consciousness, the bottle is the mind.
Full of jokes and humor, irreverence, warmth and profound wisdom.   ISBN 81 7261 014 9

The Search
TALKS ON THE TEN BULLS OF ZEN

The ten paintings that tell the Zen story about a farmer in search of his lost bull provide an allegorical expression of the inexpressible. Originally Taoist, they were repainted by the 12th century Chinese Zen master, Kakuan. Osho examines the deeper layers of meaning behind each painting, as well as answering questions from disciples and other seekers, in this special selection of discourses.
ISBN 3 89338 116 3

For information about visiting the Commune,
your nearest Osho Meditation Center
and general information, contact:
OSHO COMMUNE INTERNATIONAL
17 Koregaon Park, Pune 411 001 (MS), India
Tel: +91 (0) 20 628 562 Fax: +91 (0) 20 624 181
e-mail: osho-commune@osho.org

For publishing and copyright information
regarding Osho's books, contact:
OSHO INTERNATIONAL
570 Lexington Ave, New York, NY 10022, USA
Tel: +1 212 588 9888 Fax: +1 212 588 1977
e-mail: osho-int@osho.org

INTERNET
www.osho.com
A comprehensive website in different languages
featuring Osho's meditations, books and tapes,
an online tour of Osho Commune International,
a list of Osho Information Centers worldwide,
and a selection of Osho's talks.

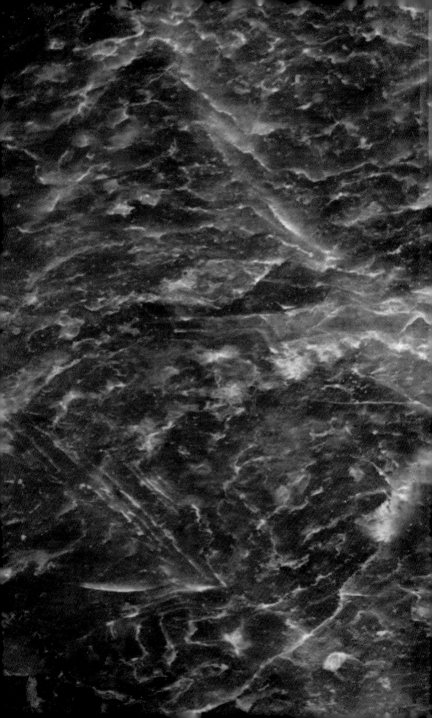